THOMAS CRANE PUBLIC LIBRARY
QUINCY MA

CITY APPROPRIATION

Dealing With Stress

Other titles in the series Life—A How-to Guide

Choosing a Community Service Career
A How-to Guide
Library ed. 978-1-59845-147-4
Paperback 978-1-59845-312-6

Friendship
A How-to Guide
Library ed. 978-0-7660-3442-6
Paperback 978-1-59845-315-7

Getting Ready to Drive
A How-to Guide
Library ed. 978-0-7660-3443-3
Paperback 978-1-59845-314-0

Volunteering
A How-to Guide
Library ed. 978-0-7660-3440-2
Paperback 978-1-59845-310-2

Getting the Hang of Fashion and Dress Codes
A How-to Guide
Library ed. 978-0-7660-3444-0
Paperback 978-1-59845-313-3

Using Technology
A How-to Guide
Library ed. 978-0-7660-3441-9
Paperback 978-1-59845-311-9

Dealing With Stress

Stress

A How-to Guide

Life
A How-to Guide

Lisa A. Wroble

Enslow Publishers, Inc.
40 Industrial Road
Box 398
Berkeley Heights, NJ 07922
USA

http://www.enslow.com

Library of Congress Cataloging-in-Publication Data

Wroble, Lisa A.
  Dealing with stress : a how-to guide / Lisa A. Wroble.
     p. cm.—(Life—a how-to guide)
  Summary: "Readers will learn about the causes of stress, how stress affects the body, and how to manage stress"—Provided by the publisher.
  Includes bibliographical references and index.
  ISBN 978-0-7660-3439-6
  1. Stress in adolescence—Juvenile literature. 2. Stress management for teenagers—Juvenile literature. 3. Teenagers—Mental health—Congresses—Juvenile literature. I. Title.
  BF724.3.S86W76 2012
  155.9'042—dc23

                         2011019282

Paperback ISBN: 978-1-59845-309-6

Printed in the United States of America

072011 Lake Book Manufacturing, Inc., Melrose Park, IL

10 9 8 7 6 5 4 3 2 1

To Our Readers: We have done our best to make sure all Internet addresses in this book were active and appropriate when we went to press. However, the author and the publisher have no control over and assume no liability for the material available on those Internet sites or on other Web sites they may link to. Any comments or suggestions can be sent by e-mail to comments@enslow.com or to the address on the back cover.

♻ Enslow Publishers, Inc., is committed to printing our books on recycled paper. The paper in every book contains 10% to 30% post-consumer waste (PCW). The cover board on the outside of each book contains 100% PCW. Our goal is to do our part to help young people and the environment too!

Illustration Credits: © 2011 Clipart.com, a division of Getty Images. All rights reserved., p. 7; LifeART © 1998 Williams & Wilkins, A Waverly Company. All rights reserved., p. 24; © Lisa Wroble, pp. 32, 35, 50, 56, 97; © 2011 Photos.com, a division of Getty Images. All rights reserved., pp. 30, 33, 40, 42, 58, 61, 74, 85, 90, 95, 100, 110; Shutterstock.com, pp. 3, 6, 8, 11, 14, 17, 22, 26, 27, 28, 29, 34, 37, 38, 46, 48, 52, 64, 66, 68, 72, 76, 78, 81, 82, 87, 88, 92, 96, 101, 104, 107, 112.

Cover Illustration: Shutterstock.com (stressed teen boy with books).

Contents

Teens Under Pressure

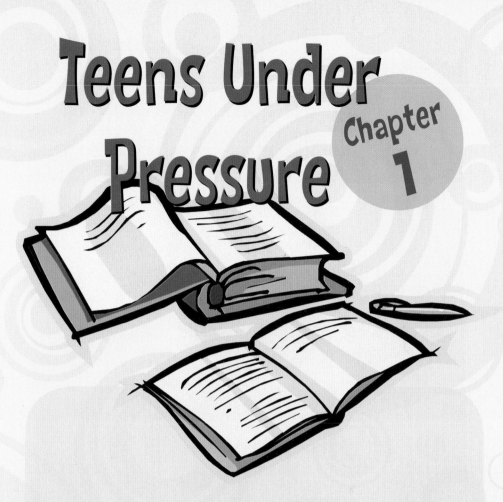

The school year had almost ended for Tyler. He was a freshman in high school and ready for a break. He and his friends were making plans and, of course, that led to drama with their girlfriends, he explains. Then he learned that his family would be moving to Florida. High school is hard enough, but having to make all new friends, adjust to a new house, a new town, and a new school was too much! But that wasn't all. The teachers started assigning more work. Every class had extra work, projects, papers, and quizzes.

A fight with a parent can be a
major source of stress for a teen.

Dealing With Stress

What Causes Stress for Teens Today?

According to research conducted by psychologists in Minnesota and Maryland, teens deal with problems at home, at school, at work, and with friends. Top stressors include:

- Homework
- Tests
- Conflicts with teachers
- Arguments with parents
- Getting along with siblings
- Chores
- Divorce
- Illness of family member
- Juggling a job and schoolwork
- Juggling sports or after-school activities
- Helping friends with problems
- Pressure from friends to try drugs, alcohol, or sex
- Planning for future (job, career, college)

"When we complained, they said it was preparing us for next year and that in the future we'd have to deal with college and job expectations," said Tyler, who also had taken a part-time job to save money for his summer plans. "I didn't know what to focus on first so I ended up just sleeping a lot," which led to more stress because the schoolwork was not getting done. "What a way to end the school year and say good-bye!" he said.[1]

"**A**s young adults we face situations that are real and painful. We do not yet have the tools that we need to deal with them because it is our first time in life when we face daily challenges. I think parents and teachers already know this but they just forgot what it was like not having any answers and perhaps they could be more sensitive about all of it when dealing with their child or student."

— *Sara, age 19, Naples, Florida*[2]

Stress—this word might make stomachs tighten or muscles tense. Those are reactions to stress. Stress is how our bodies respond to anything seen as a threat. Triggers, or causes of stress, are all around us. They are called stressors. People, places, events, and situations can all cause stress.

Stress affects every part of life. At home, hassles with parents cause stress. Fights with brothers and sisters might cause extra tension. A study of Baltimore, Maryland, teens found "family conflicts usually involved doing their homework, cleaning their room, and doing chores."[3] At school, tests, homework, and teachers cause anxiety. Coaches, tutors, and bosses add to pressures teens face. Sometimes it is a mix of these things.

Dealing With Stress

Seventeen-year-old Margot, a high-school senior, says she gets emotional when she is stressed with too much to do. "I feel angry when I have lots of schoolwork to do but have to pick my brothers up from a game."[4]

Often stress happens when we already feel overloaded. We do not feel in control of everything we have to do. This is why we think of stress as bad. But good things can cause stress too.

One of several stress-causing issues teens face is keeping the peace with their siblings.

A new job, getting a scholarship, or winning a tournament adds pressure to succeed. Getting accepted to college means adjusting to change. Even getting married can cause stress.

Stress is the body's reaction to danger. When you step off the curb and see a car speeding straight for you, you feel fear. Fear triggers adrenaline, so your heart races, and your brain sends signals to jump out of the way. The car passes. You are back on the curb, safe. But your heart will still beat fast until the brain and body are sure the danger has passed.

This is a physical response. But emotions are mixed in as well. When fifteen-year-old Megan feels stressed she says, "I get a really big attitude or I get really sad. I often cry or yell."[5]

Stress and Adolescence

The many challenges of the teen years add to stress. "Adolescence is the extraordinary period of dynamic change when a person moves from childhood to adulthood," according to a 2007 report from the Office of the U.S. Surgeon General. "During this transition, adolescents must cope with dramatic changes in their bodies, feelings, perspectives, and environments." The report discusses the stresses teens face due to being teens. They are caught between friends and family even as they move toward self-reliance, the report explains. "They will experience unfamiliar situations, pressures, desires, and challenges for which they have no prior frame of reference and often are not fully prepared to deal with effectively on their own."[6]

Dealing With Stress

Doctors and psychologists have studied stress in children and teens. All children must deal with the challenges of growing, explains human development specialist Dr. Aaron T. Ebata. Going through puberty is hard. Hormones are causing tangible changes, such as growth of body hair, acne, vocal changes, and developing bodies. "What you see on the outside is nothing compared to what is going on inside the body," says Dr. Hunter Leake III, retired pediatrician and professor of Human Growth and Development.[7] Adolescents must cope with new feelings along with these physical changes. Add to this the wishes of parents, teachers, and friends. Balancing it all is demanding. "And some kids may have to deal with things that their peers don't have to face, such as the death of a family member or moving to a new town. Most children meet these challenges successfully and grow into healthy adults. Others have a harder time coping with their problems."[8]

In addition to the challenges of growing, life changes, such as a new school, divorce, or the loss of a pet or loved one, add to stress. This type of stressor centers around not knowing what to expect. A new routine or grief over loss creates feelings of uncertainty. This doubt builds tension, which triggers stress.

Stress Is Personal

Everyone feels stress differently. We handle it differently too. "I get stomach problems and I just don't want to deal with anyone," says fourteen-year-old Candace. "I deal with stress by trying to block everything out."[9]

How Teens Define Stress

Teens know they are stressed. Stress is part of daily life. But what exactly is stress? The definitions offered are as varied as the things that cause stress. For today's teens, stress is all of the following:

"Any situation that causes someone to feel anxious, nervous, worried, or agitated. Positive stress: a situation that produces feelings of excitement, high energy, or an 'adrenaline rush.'"

> *— Margot, age 17, high-school senior*

"Feelings of uneasiness that cause a disruption in my life."

> *— Sara, age 19, part-time student*

"Something that tags along with something called pressure."

> *— Jessica, age 14, high-school freshman*

"Too many things to do all at once, feeling overwhelmed."

> *— Candace, age 14, high-school freshman*

Many teens feel overwhelmed by the amount of homework they have to do.

"When I'm overloaded with things like schoolwork and problems."

— Shelby, age 14, high-school freshman

"Being anxious. I'm anxious a lot."

— Caroline, age 14, high-school sophomore

"When you're under pressure and like, freaked out."

— Senae, age 14, high-school freshman

"Something that makes things complicated or frustrating."

— Ashley, age 15, high school sophomore

"To me stress is when you are having a bad mood or have too much going on. Being shy can also make you stressed out."

— Watson, age 19, first-semester college freshman

"Stress is tension from feelings that other people give to you."

— Colvin, age 13, middle-school student

"Stress comes from school, worrying about grades, and when people yell at me."

— Dylan, age 12, middle-school student[10]

Our reaction is based on how we view life. One person may see certain people, places, things, or events as stressful. Another person may not. Yet another person may feel only a little stress.

"One source of frequently cited family stress involved worrying about the well-being of family members," reported researchers Anita Chandra and Ameena Batada.[11] The report stated that 50 percent of boys in the study worried about younger siblings. Only 35 percent of girls in the study felt stress over worry about siblings.

What about stress over friends? As they learn to be independent, teens bounce between the support of family and deepening friendships. Stress and worry play their part. Among teens who were part of a study called Shifting the Lens, 58 percent of girls said they worried about friends. But only 33 percent of the boys did.[12]

Just as everyone views stressors differently, everyone handles stress differently too. Dealing with stress depends on our perception. It depends on whether we see a stressor as harmful or not. It depends on whether we see it as a problem or as a challenge to conquer.

Dealing with stress begins with understanding what stress is and how it affects us. Then we can learn coping skills to help us deal with it effectively.

According to Dr. Jennifer Dyl, psychologist at Bradley Hospital in Rhode Island, "Since adolescence is a period of significant changes, including physical, emotional, social, and academic changes, many teens are under more stress than at any other time of life."[13]

Dealing With Stress

The Body on High Alert

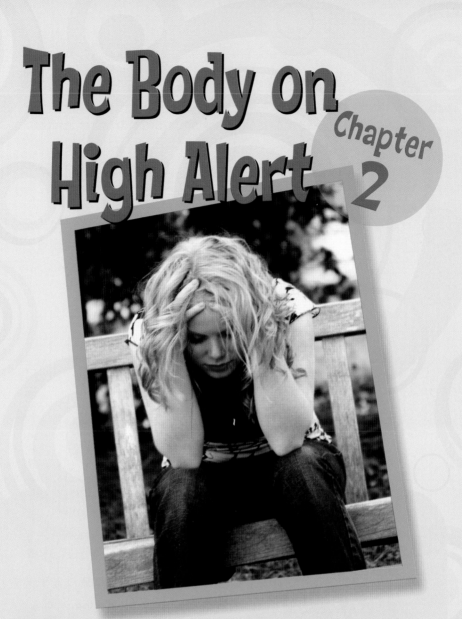

What is stress? A survey of high-school students in southwest Florida showed that many teens do not understand stress. They describe it as something that causes anxiety or something that makes life difficult.[1] They are close. They are describing stressors, or stress triggers. Feeling stressed is a gut reaction to a stress trigger.

Stress begins with the body's reaction to a stressor, which is something that triggers a stress response. It could be a person, thing, event, feeling, or situation. Stress is anything that causes alarm. The mind and body then react to the threat.

The reaction is instant. Harm or danger is expected, so the body goes on high alert. Once that threat has passed, the body returns to normal. It relaxes. This reaction to stress is called allostasis. It is both a physical and an emotional reaction to stress. Allostasis is the cycle of reacting to and then recovering from stress.

How the Body Reacts

During the stress response the body goes on "high alert." It prepares for danger. To provide more energy where the body needs it, some systems shut down. Others speed up.

- Breathing goes up.
- Heart rate goes up.
- The body's ability to fight off infection or illness increases in the short term but slows down during ongoing stress.
- The digestive system slows down.
- The reproductive system is suppressed.

Dealing With Stress

How Stress Affects the Body

In allostasis, the body goes through three stages: (1) alarm, (2) resistance, and (3) exhaustion.

Suppose you are walking home from school with a group of friends. You've made this journey every school day for five years. You know the first two streets you walk down are in the school zone with crossing guards watching traffic for you. As your group enters the street to cross at the corner outside the school zone, you drop a book. You bend and pick it up and then, without looking, step into the intersection to catch up. A car honks. You jump back but still feel the whoosh of air as the car passes. Your friends have turned to see what caused the commotion, and they gaze at you, stunned.

This situation caused stress for both the student and the driver. The initial reaction is alarm: "I am going to get hit by a car" or "I am going to run into that student." The brain sends signals for the body to react. The student jumps back. The driver honks and swerves to miss the student.

While this all happens in a split second, a lot is happening in the body. The body prepares to either flee danger or face a challenge. This is known as the "fight or flight" response. If we view the situation as very dangerous, we will respond intensely. If we see it as only causing possible discomfort, we respond less intensely. It all depends on what we feel as "danger."

Whether we react intensely or not, the alarm stage is the first stage of stress.

The "Fight or Flight" Response

The stress response came about as a way of creating quick energy in the face of physical danger. You have probably noticed it in animals. When an animal is scared, it tries to run away. If it is cornered, it will attack. In humans the basic response is the same. The body prepares to do one of two things: run or face the danger.

This "fight or flight" response is the first stage of allostasis. It is a personal response because it is partly based on experience. Allostasis begins in the brain, according to professor and brain researcher Bruce McEwen.[2] When we walk into a new school, give an oral report, or are approached by a stranger, our brain sets to work. It searches our experiences to decide if this situation might be a threat. Have we had a similar experience? If so, what happened? How did it feel? Can we cope with it now?

> "The most stressful experience I have ever had was when I had to drive my mom to the hospital. I was only in high school and so worried that I had a panic attack."
>
> —— Samantha, age 18, Naples, Florida[3]

The goal of the stress response is to keep the body safe. Many things happen at once in the body. The priority becomes a shift in energy to help deal with the immediate situation. It is much like preparing for a hurricane or snowstorm. We pull together supplies in case power goes out and roads are blocked. We find flashlights, candles, and batteries. We gather canned food, and fill jugs or the bathtub with water. We are ready for whatever happens.

Stress Hormones

The brain and body work together rapidly. Deep in the brain the hypothalamus sounds the high alert. It signals the adrenal glands, which sit on top of the kidneys. To allow an instant response, the hypothalamus uses a path of nerves that goes directly to the adrenal glands. The adrenal glands dump stress hormones into the bloodstream.

The first is epinephrine, also called adrenaline. This makes the pulse race. The heart pumps harder and faster to send extra blood to the muscles and organs. The adrenaline flowing through the body alerts other organs. Bronchial tubes in the lungs dilate, or open up. This allows more oxygen to rush into the lungs. More oxygen also reaches the brain. This is important to keep us alert.

Adrenaline also causes the tiny muscle at the shaft of each hair follicle to contract. It makes a bump which we call a goose bump, and our hair stands on end. This keeps us warm

The adrenal glands, which are located on top of the kidneys, release adrenaline and other hormones when a person is stressed.

Dealing With Stress

internally, explains Dr. Leake.[4] Epinephrine, or adrenaline, also makes the blood vessels feeding the skin smaller, so blood flow to the skin is limited. If we get a shallow cut we will not bleed as much. Adrenaline also causes the release of proteins and other elements in our blood plasma to speed up blood clotting. This is another defense against losing too much blood if injured. To keep the body working during the stress crisis, the brain also releases natural painkillers. They are called endorphins.

While all of this is happening, the brain sends another message. This time it uses hormones to send it. The hypothalamus makes corticotropin-releasing factor, or CRF. CRF acts on the pituitary gland, an almond-sized gland at the front of the brain. The pituitary gland makes adrenocorticotropic hormone, or ACTH. It sends it through the bloodstream to the adrenal glands.

Next, the ACTH travels to the outer layer of the adrenal glands. ACTH causes the adrenal glands to create glucocorticoids. Glucocorticoids supply instant energy. They also suppress the body's immune system.

Cortisol

The adrenal glands also turn cholesterol into cortisol. This is one of the helpful ways the body uses cholesterol. The body's energy stores are used up during the adrenaline rush. Cortisol works in the liver to spur release of the body's principal fuel—glucose.

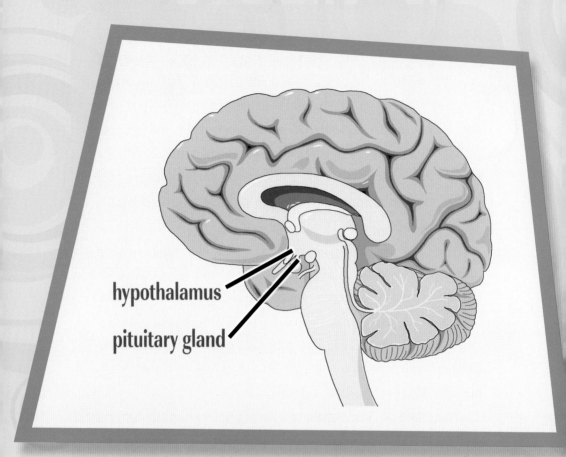

hypothalamus

pituitary gland

The hypothalamus and pituitary gland work together to activate the adrenal glands' release of glucocorticoids.

Cortisol also works as a brake in the immune system. It stops the immune system from causing inflammation if tissue is damaged. Less inflammation means that muscles can move more freely, and there is less pain. In addition, cortisol makes the red blood cells more likely to clot, and it also changes the texture of white blood cells by making them sticky. They can

Dealing With Stress

cling to blood vessel walls and to body tissues. They are the body's main defense against infection and injury, making repairs wherever they are needed. When there is loss of blood, the release of cortisol is a possible lifesaving response.

But with too much cortisol, bad things begin to happen. It blocks the work of insulin. Insulin stimulates muscle to use glucose for energy. Excess cortisol encourages the storing of body fat. Such body fat usually becomes belly fat. At high amounts it takes protein from muscle and changes it into fat. It can also cause minerals to be lost from bone. Bones break more easily.[5] Too much cortisol can shut down the immune system, making the body defenseless against illness.

In the short term, cortisol is helpful. In the long term, when too much builds up, the body suffers. "The problem with stress arises when the body cannot turn off the cycle started by ACTH," according to certified nutritionist Phyllis A. Balch.[6] "Ordinarily, cortisol is broken down during sleep, and is replenished every morning. When stress is unremitting, the body goes out of balance."

Normally, once danger has passed, the body relaxes. But if the stress goes on too long, the body moves into the second stage. It can happen if the body is feeling physical distress— treading water while waiting for help, for example, or running a race that is longer than you trained for. It can also happen during constant low-grade stress too, such as dealing with bullies every day at school. Even living with extremes of heat or cold can cause the body to go into the second stage.

The Body on High Alert

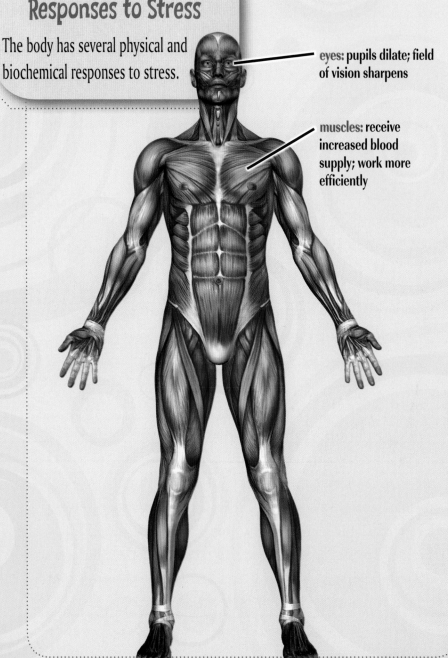

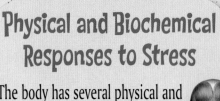

Physical and Biochemical Responses to Stress

The body has several physical and biochemical responses to stress.

eyes: pupils dilate; field of vision sharpens

muscles: receive increased blood supply; work more efficiently

26

Dealing With Stress

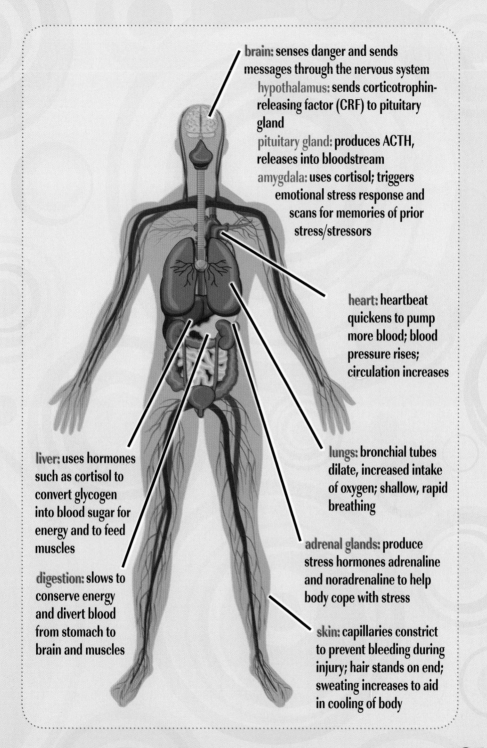

brain: senses danger and sends messages through the nervous system

hypothalamus: sends corticotrophin-releasing factor (CRF) to pituitary gland

pituitary gland: produces ACTH, releases into bloodstream

amygdala: uses cortisol; triggers emotional stress response and scans for memories of prior stress/stressors

heart: heartbeat quickens to pump more blood; blood pressure rises; circulation increases

liver: uses hormones such as cortisol to convert glycogen into blood sugar for energy and to feed muscles

digestion: slows to conserve energy and divert blood from stomach to brain and muscles

lungs: bronchial tubes dilate, increased intake of oxygen; shallow, rapid breathing

adrenal glands: produce stress hormones adrenaline and noradrenaline to help body cope with stress

skin: capillaries constrict to prevent bleeding during injury; hair stands on end; sweating increases to aid in cooling of body

The Body on High Alert

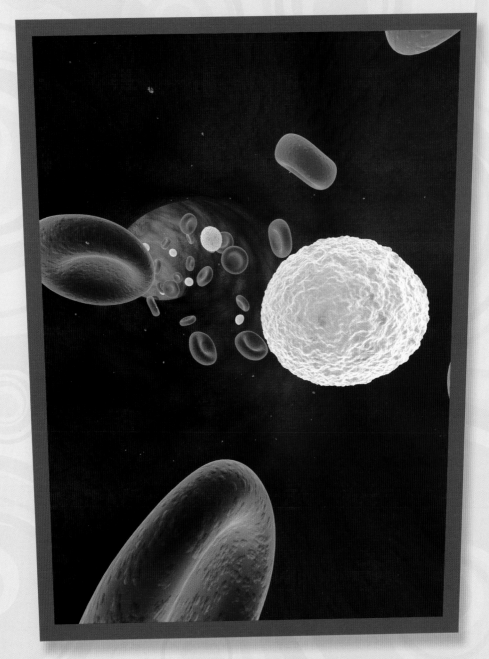

White blood cells, also called leukocytes, fight off infections and repair damaged tissue.

Dealing With Stress

This stage is called resistance, according to professor and researcher Bruce McEwen, who tracks how the brain works with the body.[7] McEwen explains that during this stage, the body starts to fight against the stressor. During the resistance stage, the body may not be able to handle any new problems. New stressors may cause slow or little reaction. The body cannot physically cope with anything more. This is one reason people often become ill when facing ongoing stress.

If the stress continues, the body loses its ability to respond. The body wears out from being on alert too long. This is the third stage. It is called the stage of exhaustion.

"Today, most of our stresses are not the result of physical threats, but the body still responds as if they were," explains Balch.[8] We may not have to worry about wild animals hunting us for food as people did in prehistoric times or about the bubonic plague that wiped out millions in medieval Europe, but modern life has its own hardships to which the body must react and keep us safe.

Who Needs Stress?

Humans need stress. Surprised? The truth is, we do not function well without stress. We often think of stress as the pressures, conflicts, and troubles in life. But not all stress is bad. Goals, for example, add pressure. But they also help us move forward. Deadlines help us get projects done. Stress stirs life up. It presents challenges and provides opportunities.

Stress is the body's reaction to danger, discomfort, or change. Running late causes a mild stress response. Forgetting to do a homework assignment might cause more stress. One student may view this as mild stress. Another student may feel extremely stressed. We each react differently. There are different types of stress. Understanding how we see and feel about each is the key to coping with stress.

Having a little stress is good. It helps us push ourselves to do well in school and at sports. It helps us look good in our jobs. Without that pressure we may not study to get better grades. We might not finish school projects. We might not go to practice daily. Without a little pressure, we may not even get to work or school on time.

Types of Stress

A little stress keeps us on the lookout, ready to meet a challenge. The nervous system is designed to meet that pressure. Then it quickly returns to normal. It relaxes and waits for the next challenge. This is positive stress.

Another type of helpful stress is called eustress. It is the reaction we feel as our body prepares for "fight or flight." The heart, mind, and muscles are ready for the strength needed to meet the challenge ahead. Our pulse quickens, muscles tense, perspiration increases. We are alert and ready for action. We have energy. We are motivated to do our best. Anyone playing sports draws on eustress during games. People who perform in front of crowds, such as figure skaters, dancers, gymnasts, musicians, actors, and singers, draw on eustress.

Categories of Stress

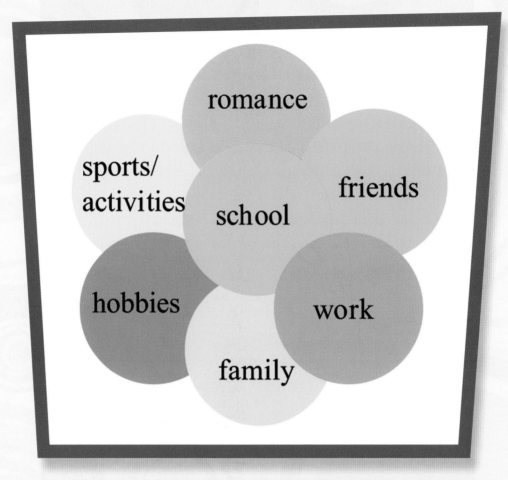

Many teens categorize their stress as coming from parents, teachers, peers, bosses, and friends. Sometimes the categories overlap, as in the diagram above. For example, you might work with a classmate (overlapping school and work) or take a romantic interest in a friend's sibling (overlapping friends and romance).

Dealing With Stress

Eustress is also the type of stress used in solving problems and working creatively. Surgeons, cooks, store employees, bus drivers, business and office workers, artists, and authors all draw on eustress. The body creates extra energy for motivation, inspiration, and strength to perform well. You will also feel this type of stress when you watch an exciting movie or go on rides at a theme park.

When a little stress turns into a lot of stress, it leads to bad stress. The body responds to pressure as if it were in a "fight or flight" situation. Bad stress is what we tend to think of when we hear the word *stress*.

Bad stress can be either acute or chronic. Acute stress is intense. Emergencies are examples of acute stress. It puts our bodies on high alert. But it also passes quickly.

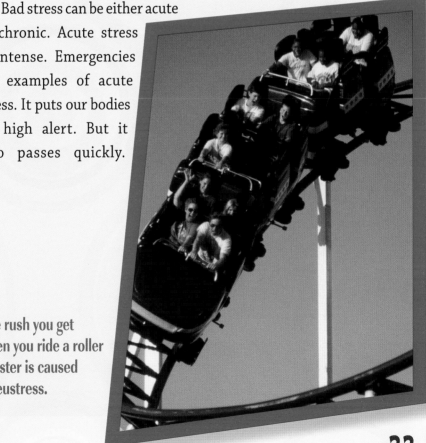

The rush you get when you ride a roller coaster is caused by eustress.

So the body responds to stress and then relaxes. Only when the body is constantly facing acute stressors does this type of stress become bad. The body is on a roller coaster of stress. It responds and relaxes, responds to new stress, and relaxes.

When stress goes on for too long, it becomes chronic. The body never has a chance to relax. This can lead to over-stress. "A 'pile up' of many stressful life events in a small amount of time is more difficult for adolescents than dealing with just one event," explains Ebata.[1] Such a pileup can cause over-stress. The body shuts down as it becomes exhausted. Or it cannot deal with new stresses. Then we become ill or get injured.

Distress is another type of stress. It is mild stress. The body feels discomfort more than danger, but it still responds with alarm. "I am not ready for this test!" or "The line to the restroom is too long. I can't wait!" Distress moves beyond physical stress. The emotions are involved too as we think about the consequences. We might feel frustrated or fearful. When we are unable to deal with anger, distress sets in. Like other types of stress, distress can be acute or chronic. If it goes on too long, anxiety can develop. Anxiety is a type of chronic distress.

People feel differently about each stressor in their lives. So it is important to understand how stress affects you. How much can you handle? Sometimes it goes on for a longer time than is helpful to the body. Since stress also affects emotions, it takes a toll on our physical and mental well-being.

Dealing With Stress

It helps to think of stress as a rubber band, according to Frederic Friedman of Lifespan's division of behavioral and preventive medicine. "With no tension on the band, it doesn't function at all," he explains. "With too much tension, it breaks. When taut for a long time, it loses its elasticity."[2] Do you know how much stress you can handle? Can we learn from stress?

Human Performance Curve

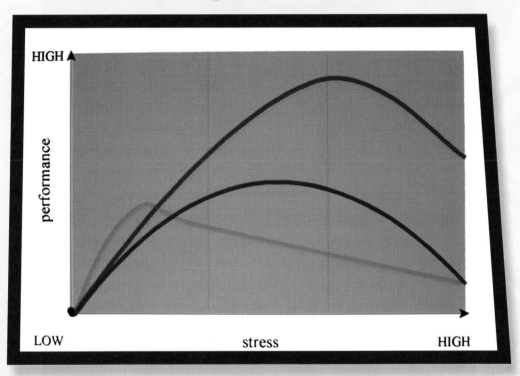

We do need a little stress in our lives to ensure we are challenged and perform at our optimum levels. The key is in maintaining balance, as in the green line. The red line indicates too much stress, while the yellow line shows a listless and unchallenged person.

Thirteen-year-old Colvin believes we learn from stress because in learning to deal with it, we grow and become better people. "Since second grade I've liked to express my feelings on paper by drawing or to express my emotions on the soccer field, which gets rid of tension. I forget about stuff going on at home or school, like a bad grade on a test, and get lost in the game or making art. Afterward, I feel better." He says these are positive results of coping and believes they will help him continue learning to deal with stress without the help of parents or teachers.[3]

Seventeen-year-old Margot believes good can come out of stress. "It forces you to learn to prioritize and organize your life. It pushes you to mature and deal with not-so-desirable situations." She also describes how it helps her work harder toward her skating goals. A three-minute skating routine is tiring and physically demanding. If she does not prepare for it, or allows herself to get out of shape, it is also painful. She compares learning from stress as similar to her training. "Persevering through stressful situations is like training your emotional skills to perform well under pressure."[4]

The Good and Bad of Stress

There are five major types of stressors: (1) physical changes, (2) our environment, (3) life situations, (4) behaviors, and (5) mental efforts. Illness can create physical stressors. So can pushing our muscles beyond their limits or doing something that risks injury. Noise, overcrowding, abandonment, being too

Dealing With Stress

hot or too cold, and natural disasters can trigger environmental stress. Life situations that cause stress include poverty, single-parent households, death of a friend or relative, and being surrounded by strangers. Behaviors that can create stressors include smoking, drinking, poor diet, and lack of exercise. Taking a test, struggling to learn something, or concentrating for a high video game score can trigger mental stress.

There are many ways to cope with stress. Some people read to forget about their problems for a while. Others might like to exercise, paint, listen to music, or play sports.

Who Needs Stress?

Learning something new or concentrating to achieve are not bad. These are examples of how stress is needed in life. Even the stressor of being too hot or too cold causes us to change the situation. But sometimes one stressor triggers more stressors (for example, when poverty causes a poor diet), and we feel overwhelmed. This is when stress becomes bad.

When our reaction to a stressor helps us get something done, it is good stress. When it makes us so fearful, anxious, or unable to take action, it becomes bad stress. When stress goes on too long, it can cause other health problems.

Though it may feel good at the time, eating a lot of junk food and vegging out on the couch too often will stress your body in the long run.

Dealing With Stress

Rate Your Stress Potential

Number a sheet of paper from 1 to 10. Read each question. Write down the rating for how often you feel this way. Honestly answer the following questions.

	Never	Rarely	Sometimes	Often	Always
1. I lose sleep worrying or wake several times during the night.	0	1	2	3	4
2. I yell, throw things, or scream when I feel overwhelmed.	0	1	2	3	4
3. I feel angry, worried, or hurt over minor problems.	0	1	2	3	4
4. I smoke, drink, or use drugs to help me forget problems.	0	1	2	3	4
5. I have too much to do all the time or feel rushed to finish projects.	0	1	2	3	4
6. I catch colds, flu, or get sick a lot.	0	1	2	3	4
7. My school grades or work have gotten worse lately.	0	1	2	3	4
8. I feel restless, bored, or do not care about things I used to care about.	0	1	2	3	4
9. I have trouble making decisions or setting priorities.	0	1	2	3	4
10. I grind my teeth, get headaches, stomachaches, skin breakouts, tight neck or shoulder muscles, have a racing heart or trouble breathing.	0	1	2	3	4

Find your score: Add the numbers on your sheet. Your score shows your stress potential.

15 or less: You have little stress in your life. When you do have stress, you handle it well. Consider what you are doing and why it is working. Then keep doing it.

16-29: You face stress every day. You do a good job handling stress, but you can learn better ways to cope. Be sure to take breaks. Learn what stresses you out most so you can take action to limit how it affects you.

30-40: You have a lot of stress in your life. Or you have just a little but do not cope with it. Learn about what stresses you and how to react. This will guide you toward areas for learning coping skills.

Chapter 4 What Stresses You Out?

Stress is subjective. That is, people feel stress differently. Different things are seen as stressful. What one person sees as harmful is not perceived that way by someone else. What upsets one person is nothing unusual to another. We most often learn our stress perception from our families. We interpret the way our parents—or an adult

40

Dealing With Stress

we respect—react to stress and assume that we should find similar situations stressful. Since we view different things as dangerous, we also react differently to stressors. Our personality affects how we react. Hormones affect how we react. So does the kind of day we are having. If we are having a good day, a pop quiz in science may not worry us. If we are having a good day, having to help a younger brother with his chores may not be a big deal. If we are having a bad day, both of those things could really upset us.

Age and experience make a difference too. For example, nineteen-year-old Sara rates planning for the future as her top stressor. She rates it at the top because many others things that stress her tie into planning for the future.[1] A younger teen may not be worrying about that yet. Fifteen-year-old Kelsey says, "I'm not entirely sure where my life is going, and this stresses me out sometimes. Other times, I just go with the flow and don't care too much."[2] Yet Colvin, age thirteen, and Caitlin, fourteen, both rate planning for the future high on their stress list because teachers constantly push them to think about high school, college, and careers. "I wish teachers didn't try so hard to prepare us for the future, because that only makes everything more stressful," says Caitlin.[3]

Understanding what stress means to you will help in learning to cope with it. First, learn to notice signs of stress. Second, learn how stress affects you. What stresses you a lot? What stresses you a little? Are you stressed sometimes? Or all the time?

A headache is a common symptom of too much stress.

Dealing With Stress

Researchers in the Shifting the Lens study found that teen girls and boys feel signs of stress at different levels. "Boys tended to describe physical ramifications of stress, whereas girls tended to focus on physical and emotional consequences," state Anita Chandra and Ameena Batada.[4]

Signs of Stress

Our bodies have different ways of letting us know something is wrong: low energy; trouble falling asleep or sleeping too much; loss of appetite or eating too much; headaches, stomachaches, or backaches; tight muscles in our shoulders, neck, or jaw; and teeth grinding are all signs of stress.

> "I know I'm stressed when I can't sleep at night. The thoughts will not shut off."
> —Colvin, age 13[5]

Our minds also let us know when something is wrong. Mental signs of stress include feeling restless or distracted. We are distracted when we cannot focus in school, at work, or while doing things we normally enjoy. Forgetting things or forgetting directions also happens when we are stressed.

Feeling overwhelmed or having "cluttered" thoughts about everything on our to-do list are both signs of stress. Not being able to decide what to do first can cause us to feel overwhelmed. This is how Megan, age fifteen, knows she is stressed. "I feel like I can't get anything done," she says. "I have to ask my parents to help me complete tasks and I end up staying up really late."[6]

How Do You Know You Are Feeling Stressed?

Symptoms of stress change with each person. They might vary with a situation too. When a group of Collier County (Florida) teens were asked how they knew they were "stressed out" they provided the following list:

- crankiness, easily agitated, irritability with things that should not be upsetting
- more tired than usual
- anxiety, overeating, emotions fly
- headaches, neck/shoulders get really tense, forehead scrunches, skin breaks out
- feel overwhelmed
- screaming and yelling at parents, friends, people trying to help
- crying, getting bratty
- feeling sad, getting a really big attitude

Worrying and other emotional reactions, such as feeling frustrated or "jumpy," are common when we are stressed. Thoughts that are "stuck" in our heads, worrying about past events or possible outcomes, and getting mad at ourselves are also mental signs of stress. Fourteen-year-old Caroline knows she is stressed because "[her] mind is 'moving around' in different directions, [her] hands get sweaty, and sometimes [she cries]." To deal with her stress she will "vent to [her] mom, watch TV, run, and eat."[7]

Emotional responses such as yelling and crying are normal for teens. According to the a report by the Office of the Surgeon General of the United States, parts of the brain mature at different rates. For example, the limbic areas of the brain handle emotions. The limbic areas work with the frontal lobes, which mature later. The frontal lobes "are thought to be responsible for self-regulation, judgment, reasoning, problem-solving, and impulse control" the report states. Since the timing is off between these areas of the brain, the result might be "impulsive decision and actions, a disregard for consequences, or emotional reactions that can put teenagers at serious risk in ways that may surprise even the adolescents themselves."[8]

In a survey of Florida teens, several boys indicated that breaking and throwing things or having uncontrollable anger were ways they reacted when stressed. "I crashed my remote airplane and my older brother laughed at me. That made me mad, so I wailed on him [with the broken plane]. Then my dad yelled at both of us," says Brent, age fifteen. "The worst part was I could have fixed the plane, until I destroyed it on my brother."[9]

Degrees of Stress

How often do you feel stressed? Is it acute or mild? Acute stress arises out of alarm. We often have to take immediate action. Mild stress is not so intense. You do not have to act right now.

A good cry can often help teens relieve some frustration, but frequent emotional outbursts may be a sign that they should talk to someone.

Dealing With Stress

You have time to consider how to deal with a problem. But the body still reacts to keep you alert and safe in case you get injured.

These two scenarios show the difference. Suppose you are in a big city with your school dance team for a competition. Your team won a ribbon, and everyone is happy. Happiness turns into rowdiness as you all wait for the commuter train to get to the airport.

Scene 1: Acute stress. As the train heads toward the platform, you are pushed toward the edge. You start to lose your balance. You think you will fall but your best friend grabs your arm. You are safe. Both of you feel an intense stress response: sweating, flushed skin, beating heart, dry mouth, and bristled hair. As the danger passes, you begin to relax.

Scene 2: Mild stress. As the train heads toward the platform, everyone pushes to grab their bags. You are shoved away from the train by other passengers. You push your way back to the group and see your bag. As you grab it and head toward the doors, they close. The train pulls away. You are left alone in a strange city. Now what will you do?

Your body probably reacted with alarm as you were pushed away from the crowd. But you were not in immediate danger. As you are left alone, your may feel fear or panic. Your heart pounds and you feel sweaty, but you are not harmed. Your body relaxes—but just a little. You are no longer on high alert, but you will have to face this problem. You will need energy. You will need an alert mind. You are still stressed, but it is mild. It is passive stress.

Sometimes we feel passive stress for long periods of time. This becomes low-grade stress. Our body keeps the stress hormones flowing though we do not feel alarm or danger. When low-grade stress goes on for too long, it can cause health problems. Signs of low-grade stress include anxiety, restlessness, eating disorders, melancholy, and decreased self-esteem.

"Stress can be either acute or long-term. Long-term stress is particularly dangerous," explains nutritionist Phyllis A. Balch.[10] Ongoing stress wears out the body. She explains that stress changes our immune system. This makes it easier for us to become ill. It also slows healing.

"Chronic stress, or stress left unchecked or unmanaged, can have a profound impact on an adolescent's physical and mental well-being, leading to illnesses such as depression," according to researchers Chandra and Batada.[11]

Stress Load

Sometimes we are not aware of how many stressors we are facing. Sometimes we are not aware of how complicated life has become. We often do not notice the signals our body and mind are sending. Learning to tune in can help us begin to cope with the stress in our lives. Become aware of how you feel when you are stressed.

Do you feel tired or cranky? Do you break out in hives? Get a headache? Suffer from digestive problems? Each of these symptoms relates to a part of the body involved in the stress response. We see different things as stressful, so we react differently to stress. We have different stress loads. Stress load is our tolerance for stress.

During the high alert of "fight or flight," it is clear we are stressed. Our body prepares to take action. But some stressors cause a passive response. We can consider ways to solve a problem, such as how to get everyone to do their part in a group project. Or we can ignore the stressor, such as someone blaring the radio or TV next door when we are trying to study.

Passive stress does tax the body, though. Some people may feel cranky or tired. When they ignore signs of hunger, blood sugar drops, and with it, energy for the body to use. Others get fever blisters or hives when they are stressed. The skin is the passive stress organ in this situation. Signals for stress target this vulnerable, or unprotected, part of the body.

Where Do You Harbor Stress?

Stress can cause fatigue, chronic headaches, irritability, changes in appetite, memory loss, low self-esteem, withdrawal, teeth grinding, cold hands, high blood pressure, shallow breathing, nervous twitches, insomnia or other changes in sleep patterns, and/or gastrointestinal disorders.

What Stresses You Out?

Quadrants of Stress

	Positive	Negative
Mild	A temporarily stressful situation we've chosen. • performing a solo at the dance recital • giving a speech in front of the entire school	A temporarily stressful situation. • being chased by a Doberman • discovering your new boyfriend's ex-girlfriend is now in your science class
Severe	Ongoing stress for an activity or situation we have some control over. • an exercise plan or conditioning • practice for sports competition • pushing toward a personal goal	Ongoing, intense stress. • dealing with a chronic illness • dealing with divorce • being bullied at school

Learn to identify the type of stress you are feeling. Remember that some stress is positive because it serves to challenge us to do better. Other stress that comes from conflict or prolonged problems, or that leads to stomachaches or headaches, is negative stress.

For many people, the target spots for stress are written into their genes. Allergies, asthma, and high blood pressure may run in families. Skin problems such as eczema, psoriasis, acne, and hives may be inherited. Stress can make them worse. Sometimes stress creates these trouble areas.

Stress hormones send messages between the brain, glands, and organs in the body. The hypothalamus and pituitary gland in the brain and the adrenal glands on top of the kidneys work together. This is called the hypothalamic-pituitary-adrenal (HPA) axis. They work together like players on a soccer team. Two players relay the ball back and forth, which sets up for a third player to make a goal. When the play is timed properly, the goal is achieved. Likewise, the HPA axis keeps the nervous system, glands, and immune system in balance. "When the HPA axis is functioning properly, we have the energy and focus to deal with a crisis," explains Bruce McEwen.[12] If the axis tilts out of balance, the target spot gets overloaded. We might get severe headaches or catch a cold that will not go away. Stress that goes on too long tilts the HPA axis. How much it takes to tilt that axis depends on stress load.

Stress Perception

How much can we take? How positive are we about stressors? Our personality has a lot to do with it. Psychologist Suzanne Kobasa uses the term "hardiness" to describe how well we respond to stress. Hardiness includes three elements: commitment, control, and openness to challenge.[13]

Dealing with acne is a normal part of being a teenager, but stress can cause worse than usual breakouts. Stress causes hormonal changes that throw your body out of balance and aggravate already present skin problems.

Commitment relates to how we see ourselves. Do you believe in yourself? How much do you value yourself? If we have strong commitment, we like who we are and we know we can deal with the tasks we are given.

Control relates to the action we believe we can take to face events. Do you believe you can change things in your life? What steps can you take for a different result?

Openness to challenge is about growth. Do you see problems as a threat or something to overcome? Are you willing to see opportunity in the stresses you face? Do you believe good can come out of stress?

Kobasa did research on her idea of stress hardiness. It showed that people with commitment, control, and openness to challenge handled stress well. People who were hardy had fewer illnesses from stress than less hardy people.[14]

Coping Skills

Can people learn to be hardier? Yes. Each time we cope with a stressor we are better able to handle it next time we are faced with it. Learning skills to handle stress can help. So can taking better care of ourselves. And that means in mind and body.

Ebata explains: "There are two major ways to cope with stress. One way is PROBLEM SOLVING. This involves trying to deal with the problem by changing the situation or getting rid of the problem. Another way of handling stress is MANAGING EMOTIONS. This involves handling the thoughts and feelings caused by the problem."[15]

Ebata has a term for those who are hardy: well-adjusted. These are people who find solutions to problems. They look on the bright side when they are in difficult situations. And they have hobbies or activities they enjoy. "Acting to solve problems often requires planning. Sometimes it requires learning new skills," Ebata says. "For example, coping with poor grades might require learning study skills and making time to complete homework. Coping with feeling left out might require learning social skills. An example of seeing the positive side would be focusing on your team's good performance even though they lost the game."[16]

You can improve your skills at problem solving. Brainstorm to help think of solutions to a problem. Friends can help. Try these steps:

- First, write down what the problem is. It may be something troubling you. It may be a conflict with a teacher or another friend. This is called identifying the problem.

- Next, think of possible ways to deal with this problem. Do not judge these options. Even if they seem silly or impossible, list them.

- Now look at the list. Choose two or three that may work in dealing with the problem. What steps can you take to act on those ideas?

- From the list of steps, decide which solution you might try first. Some problems or stressors take more than one try to solve. Sometimes you cannot change

Dealing With Stress

the situation, but if you are prepared with possible solutions, you might get a parent or teacher to listen to your ideas and put one into action.

Nineteen-year-old Sara describes how she uses problem solving to help her deal with stress. "I have mapped out the situation in my mind or on a piece of paper. I'll ask myself questions like, 'Why are you allowing this person to make you feel this way?' and when I think of the answer, I usually have a solution and can solve my problem."[17]

Managing emotions, Ebata says, is important in dealing with problems that feel out of control. It is also important in the early stages of problem solving. He explains that it is okay to blow off steam or avoid the problem for a short time. Watching TV or listening to music are two common ways to get away from a problem. These activities distract the mind. This can be important in getting ready to face a tough problem.[18]

Assertiveness

An important coping skill relates to both problem solving and emotion. Assertiveness—standing up for yourself—is another way to face problems. Conflicts with friends, teachers, and parents are common among teens. Many of the low-grade stressors we deal with are linked with relationships. Emotions often stir up these issues. So teens especially feel the impact. Not only do adolescents need to get along with classmates and teachers, but they also begin taking romantic interest in others. Because they are also trying to become more independent, their

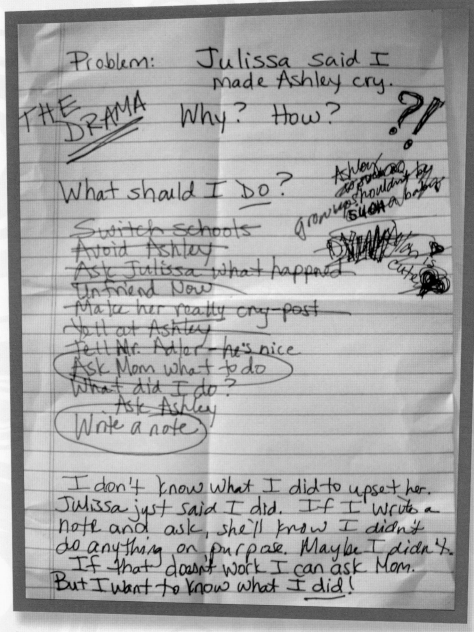

Problem: Julissa said I made Ashley cry.

THE DRAMA   Why? How? ?!

What should I DO?   Ashley shouldn't be such a baby

Switch schools
Avoid Ashley
Ask Julissa what happened
Unfriend Now
Make her really cry-post
Yell at Ashley
Tell Mr. Adler-he's nice
Ask Mom what to do
What did I do?
Ask Ashley
Write a note

I don't know what I did to upset her.
Julissa just said I did. If I write a
note and ask, she'll know I didn't
do anything on purpose. Maybe I didn't.
If that doesn't work I can ask Mom.
But I want to know what I did!

A student brainstorms possible solutions to the conflict with a friend. Writing things out can help put problems in perspective, making them easier to solve.

Dealing With Stress

relationship with family changes. When they have difficulty taking charge of these relationships, problems occur. This adds up to stress.

Assertiveness falls between aggression and compliance. Bullies are aggressive. They make demands and focus only on what they want. Aggressive people deny the rights of others. Nonaggressive people are passive. They are compliant, or bend to the will of others. They often get bossed around. Or they ignore their own needs and do for others instead, which may lead to resentment.

Assertive people are direct and clear. They know what they want and need to be happy and content. They listen and understand what others want and need. They can then think about how to meet in the middle.[19] For example, suppose you and your friends go to the mall after school every Thursday. But you heard about a new store on the other side of town. Not only do they sell pottery, but customers can also make their own pieces in a workshop that is part of the store. You have always wanted to learn about pottery. But you worry your friends will laugh at you. So you have never told them about it. You have heard other kids talk about it, and it sounds fun. Now your favorite aunt's birthday is coming up. You want to get her something special—like a bowl you make and glaze yourself.

You begin feeling angry—angry that your friends never ask what you want to do on Thursdays. You feel frustrated because your needs are not met. You resent your ideas never being heard. This is what happens when we do not stand up for our

Feeling overwhelmed? Take some time out for yourself or hang out with a friend. Taking a walk or doing some other kind of physical activity is a healthy way to unwind and release pent-up energy.

Dealing With Stress

own feelings. Resentment turns to anger. If you tell your friends what you want, and listen to why they always choose the mall on Thursdays, you will set positive problem solving in motion. When you can calmly explain why you want to try out this new shop, you may be surprised. Maybe your friends have not heard about it. Maybe they did not think anyone else in your circle of friends was interested. And maybe you can make plans to get together and try it out on a different day. But you will not know their thoughts or wants or needs unless you try to learn about them.

It is important to use assertive words. Focus on expressing your feelings. "I" phrases help: "I think we should do something else." "I feel it would be fun to try making pottery." "I want to make my aunt a ceramic bowl for her birthday." If you want to show your willingness to work with others, use phrases such as "we could" or "let's." "Let's go to the park instead." "We could see a movie." "We could all meet at my house." "Let's each do something to help plan the surprise." Practice conversations in your mind until you are comfortable using these phrases. Expressing your feelings will give you confidence in standing up for yourself in other ways.

When you stand up for yourself, remember to stay calm. Focus on your breathing so the stress will not cause your voice to shake or get loud and sound as if you are yelling. Look into the eyes of the other person. This shows your sincerity. Ask what the other person thinks. This shows your willingness to discuss solutions.[20] Standing up for yourself takes practice.

You'll gain confidence when you successfully face easier challenges first. For example, refusing a request or invitation is an easier challenge than confronting someone who is talking about you behind your back. Refuse a request by saying, "I'm sorry. I'd really like to but I can't."

Other Stress-Busters

"Another way of resolving stressful situations is to find meaning in the experience," says Ebata.[21] When we can see that something good can come out of stress it helps us cope. It also adds to our growth. Next time we will be ahead in having a positive outlook.

Finding hobbies is also very important in coping with stress—singing, dancing, drawing, sewing, knitting, writing, taking long walks. Any activity that we enjoy offers time away from a problem. This is what thirteen-year-old Colvin is doing when he plays soccer and what nineteen-year-old Watson is doing when he "shoots some hoops" with friends.[22] Taking time away from the problem "often 'recharges batteries' so the person can go back to dealing with stress," Ebata explains. Whatever activity we use to help us prepare to cope comes with a caution. Ebata states that it is important not to use these activities to avoid the problem altogether. Most stressors do not just go away.[23] Ignoring problems often causes them to get bigger. Over time the stress can increase.

Dealing With Stress

The Problem With Not Coping

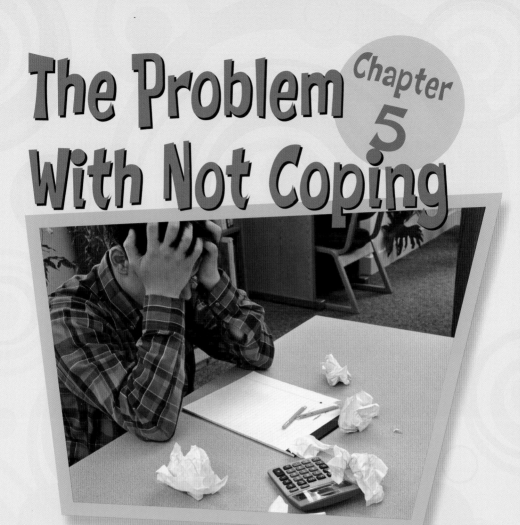

Chapter 5

Teens have a lot going on in their lives.
They are faced with new choices. These very choices create unfamiliar situations. Adolescence is a time of new experiences. When we have to do something we have never done before, it is stressful. We do not know what to expect. Looking for a first job, asking someone on a date, or learning to drive are all stressful. When we have to go somewhere we have never been, such as a new school, it can be stressful.

61

Add to that all the things we have experienced before—struggles with parents, teasing from older siblings, helping out friends, more and harder homework. It can pile up quickly. It is easy to feel stress overload. We are tempted to avoid dealing with our stress.

Researchers Anita Chandra and Ameena Batada found this among ninth grade students in their Shifting the Lens study: "The majority of teens avoided conflicts by trying to stay away from the problem, distracting themselves, or not thinking about the issue. . . . Many participants also acknowledged trying to talk to a friend or an adult about a problem to figure out how to handle stress; however, most teens did not cope with stress by talking to a nonfamily adult."[1]

Unhealthy Coping Skills

Teens need tools to face new challenges. Without tools it is difficult to know what to do. Many teens resort to the "out of sight, out of mind" method—they avoid the problem. Others avoid emotions linked to the stress. Some do both.

Reacting with anger, tears, yelling, or screaming are signs of poor coping skills. They may help blow off steam, but they do not make the stress go away. When teens resort to avoiding or ignoring stress, problems only get worse. New stresses pile up. When problems are not taken care of, it makes an emotional impact. Teens begin to feel hopeless or bad about themselves.

Though it is okay to play a video game or watch TV for a while, eventually you will have to face your stress. If doing something fun helps distract you so you come back to the problem with fresh ideas, it is a good way to cope. "Shopping is fun," says Kelsey, age fifteen, "but it doesn't cure stress. It's a distraction technique (and, might I add, it works quite nicely). But at the end of the day, you're still going to be stressed out because you haven't actually done anything about what you're stressed about."[2]

Watson, age nineteen, hangs out with his friends or goes to the park to play basketball, but Scott, age fifteen, admits he deals with stress by not dealing. "I always avoid stressful situations. If I think it's coming, I'll just walk the other way."[3] Avoiding the problem is not a healthy way to cope.

When the distractions we use to take time away from a problem through a hobby or activity turn into avoiding the problem, it is an unhealthy way to cope. Fifteen-year-old Jessica says she knows she's stressed when she craves sweets. "Desserts equal stress! I also don't talk as much as before I was stressed and I get headaches more often and I feel exhausted."[4] The stress builds because she is not really dealing with the problem or her emotions.

When playing video games, eating, or shopping does not help, some teens try more harmful things to help take their mind off stress, such as alcohol or drugs. "I've yelled and thrown things in the past. I've experimented with drugs," says Sara, age nineteen.[5] Other teens develop eating disorders or engage in self-injury behaviors.

The Problem With Not Coping

Playing video games can serve as a temporary escape from stress, but you can't avoid it forever. Your problems could get worse if they are not taken care of while they are still manageable.

Dealing With Stress

A report from the U.S. Surgeon General describes the stress teens feel just in growing up: "In graduating from elementary to middle school, from middle school to high school, and from high school to college or the workplace, adolescents move in and out of different social contexts and peer groups, which exposes them to new stressors. These transitions lead to increased responsibilities and academic expectations, which are also potential sources of stress. This is important because research shows a link between stress and alcohol consumption."[6]

Psychologist Dr. Debi Yohn adds that when children find success at an early age moving from one stage to another, they will build on this success as they move into adulthood.[7]

Aimless Coping

Without the skills to handle their stress, many teens turn to self-defeating behavior to make themselves feel better. Avoiding their stress causes ongoing stress. The body becomes taxed by the stress hormones and brain chemicals. But they have ignored the signs and done nothing about their stress.

Looking for ways to soothe the mind and settle their nerves, teens may try smoking, taking drugs, or drinking alcohol. At first they may think they feel better. The nicotine in cigarettes has a soothing effect. Alcohol relaxes the muscles. Illegal drugs may do both. But because stress hormones are surging through the bloodstream, bringing these new drugs and chemicals into the body makes the stressed body work harder.

Stress Tolerance

The word stress comes from physics. It represents the external force placed on an object. In the body, it refers to physical and emotional force. When something stretches us beyond our limits, the force needs to go somewhere.

A slingshot is a great example. Suppose you are the band on the slingshot. A rock, pulled against the band, is stress. As the band is pulled back, tension builds. It is pulled back as far as it can go. The tension grows tight. Eventually, the band must be released. The rock explodes from the slingshot. Does exploding–or getting angry–help?

What if we ignore it instead? The band is pulled back. Force builds in the taut band. If it is never released, the band weakens. But a slingshot used as it should be used works. The rock is loaded. The band is pulled back. But not beyond its limits. The band is released. It returns to normal until the next rock is loaded.

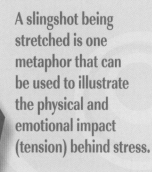

A slingshot being stretched is one metaphor that can be used to illustrate the physical and emotional impact (tension) behind stress.

For example, even small amounts of adrenaline make the heart pump harder. Cortisol is flowing through the blood and doing many different things in the body. And the lungs are taking in more oxygen to aid the muscles and keep the mind clear and alert. If a person then inhales a cigarette, nicotine makes changes in the body. Dr. Trevor Powell says nicotine "is a powerful and addictive drug that causes long-term damage to the heart and circulatory system; the tar sticks to the windpipe and inside the lungs, causing respiratory illnesses; and the carbon monoxide in the smoke is a poisonous gas."[8] Now the heart is pumping harder, the lungs are getting less oxygen into the blood, and the mind is clouded with these new chemicals.

Some teens take a different route. They take risks. Speeding and running red lights while driving, playing risk-taking games, and creating daredevil maneuvers or courses for bikes and skateboards are examples of extreme risk. Such reckless behavior creates a stress response similar to the thrill of riding a roller coaster or playing extreme sports. But remember that stress causes the immune system to prevent some natural reactions to injury. Under normal conditions, injured body parts will bleed and swell, which helps the body avoid further damage. You will not try to walk on a swollen leg or use an arm that has been badly cut. Under stress, the body turns off the swelling and limits blood loss, all to get through the danger. So playing dangerous games for the thrill of it makes the body think it is under attack. Injuries can happen without your noticing. But damage can take place that cannot be corrected.

Pulling risky stunts can be
just as addicting as drugs or alcohol
and just as likely to send you to the hospital, especially
when not wearing a helmet. Wearing safety gear when bike-riding
or skateboarding is always a good judgment call.

Dealing With Stress

(Not to mention having to explain the injuries to doctors, parents, and other authorities. They may become suspicious that you are acting recklessly or taking risks.)

Whether the avoidance behavior is smoking, drinking, drugs, or risky behavior, the body now has new stressors to deal with. Instead of doing something to stop their stress, people try to avoid it, creating more stress. Over time, the low-grade ongoing stress of aimless coping can cause serious illness. Because they do nothing to cope with their stress, people may begin to feel bad about themselves.

Feeling bad about ourselves creates self-doubt. Poor self-esteem and lack of coping skills adds to the cycle of inaction. Stresses pile up. The cycle becomes worse. Our confidence suffers. If your confidence is low, you may be easily discouraged. You might give up. This leads to feeling like a failure. If you are already avoiding stress, this will make matters even worse.

Confidence can easily spiral up or down. If you already feel good, confidence helps you do well, have a positive attitude, and feel good about yourself. If you already feel bad, you may not try hard. You question yourself. When you do not do well, negative attitudes take over. You feel worse about yourself. When we are down like this, negative comments easily enter our minds. They may be thoughts of dislike for ourselves. They may be something someone has said against you. Both play over and over in the mind, like a recording.

Psychologist Cara DiMarco explains how confidence is linked to self-trust. When confidence is low, we do not trust ourselves. Every move is examined, questioned. "You overdo healthy self-questioning to the point where you no longer question what is so but rather your own judgment. You may lack trust in your ability to perceive things correctly; to make good, clear, healthy decisions; or to be able to understand a person or an opportunity and take appropriate action. You may constantly undermine yourself by wondering 'Is this right or is that right?'"[9] To counter this cycle, teens need to improve self-esteem and learn ways to manage stress.

Boosting Self-Esteem

"Self-esteem is the ability to like yourself regardless of the feedback you receive from others," says DiMarco. When we have strong self-esteem, we worry less about what others think. We do not use only the approval of others in order to feel good. When we have strong self-esteem, we feel our opinions matter. We do not worry so much if they disagree with our views because we know that we may not agree with their opinions 100 percent either. So strong self-esteem is "the ability to enjoy and appreciate all of yourself: the strengths that you are proud of as well as the shortcomings you are aware of, the gaps between what you know how to do and what you want to be able to do."[10]

Self-esteem is seeing yourself as worthy of love and attention. It is knowing you deserve affection and respect. It is believing others care about you and show you consideration. When we have high self-esteem, it is easier to stand up for ourselves. When we stand up for what we want we are being assertive. We can tell a friend "no" if taking on one more task will make us feel overwhelmed. We can ask parents to make changes in house rules because we are getting older. We can discuss conflicts and try to solve them because we feel confident and responsible.

"One big factor determining your level of self-esteem is the quality of the self-talk that goes on in your head. Most of us have an internal tape in our head that chatters at us as we go through our day—an internal 'voice' that comments on our behavior," says DiMarco.[11]

Every minute of the day we talk with ourselves. Thoughts roll through our heads. We make plans, comments, and explore our feelings and reactions. This is our inner voice. It is self-talk. "Feelings and moods are created by thoughts about events, not by the events themselves," explains Dr. Trevor Powell.[12]

When we are stressed, we tend to focus on negative thoughts. We also draw on negative memories from the past. Both of these distort the present. Our self-talk may be altered. This leads to confused thinking. Our thoughts are not rational. For example, if you have just broken up with a boyfriend or

"**I** feel like stress is an inevitable thing that humans have to deal with. It teaches us great lessons of value that make us who we are."

—Sara, age 19[13]

The Problem With Not Coping

Having confidence, self-trust, and high self-esteem make you a well-adjusted person who can cope with stress better than someone who is always doubting himself.

Dealing With Stress

girlfriend, you will probably feel sad and upset. This mood can cause you to call up mostly bad memories. Unless you make an effort to list all the good times, your mood and thoughts turn negative. You might begin having thoughts of never finding anyone to love you again. If you stop those irrational thoughts, you can step back and see all the good things about yourself.

Like confidence, self-talk can spiral up or down. When you notice thoughts twisting toward the negative, stop yourself. Challenge the thought. Ask, what is the opposite? What is realistic? Positive self-talk helps us tap into our inner strengths. Use your mind to uncover them. Or ask friends to point out a few good qualities. Remind yourself of your strengths every day. The more you talk positively to yourself, the more able to cope with stress you will become. Look for the bright sides of situations to keep yourself feeling calmer.[14] "Keeping a positive attitude about myself and enjoying the simple pleasures of hobbies keeps me calm," says Sara, age nineteen.[15]

Another strategy linked to self-talk is visualization. Learn to see yourself getting an A on a test. Picture yourself handling a stressful situation well. Remind yourself of what you have done well in the past. As you see the "capable you" in your mind, you will come to believe in yourself.[16] Self-belief is part of confidence and self-esteem.

Positive self-esteem and self-talk, visualization, and problem solving are at the foundation of coping with stress. Understanding what stresses you and taking steps to deal with it are tools for coping. According to Chandra and Batada's Shifting the Lens study, "About one third of girls said that they used

A study revealed that boys are more likely than girls to cope with stress by playing sports.

Dealing With Stress

prevention strategies such as trying to avoid problems before they developed; however, none of the boys reported that they tried to prevent problems in this way. . . . Boys were more likely than girls to use sports as a coping mechanism."[17] Learning tools to keep the body healthy and to lessen the impact of stressors is key in managing stress.

Coping Stats

According to the Shifting the Lens study, boys and girls cope differently with stress.[18]

	Boys	Girls	
Not Coping	24% avoided or refused to deal with their stress 25% found ways to distract themselves from their stress	20% avoided or refused to deal with their stress 14% found ways to distract themselves from their stress	**Negative**
Coping	17% looked for support 35% actively tried to reduce their stress	22% looked for support 45% actively tried to reduce their stress	**Positive**

How to Manage Your Stress

Stress is all around us. A little stress is good. It helps us be our best. We cannot erase bad stress, but we can learn to limit it. Learning to manage stress can counter the effects of bad stress.

When we do not have skills for coping, our health suffers. Some teens try to avoid dealing with stress. Others try unhealthy ways of coping. But these behaviors only add to the cycle of stress. When we learn to deal with stress, we also build experience. In time, some things that used to stress us out may cause far less stress. We know we can cope with them. The body does not go into "high alert."

However strong the alert is, having a healthy body helps us deal with stress better. So does a healthy attitude—about stress in general and our ability to deal with it. Taking care of the body and mind is a starting point.

Regular Exercise

High-school students surveyed in south Florida listed physical activity as a way to deal with stress.[1] Exercise allows us to forget about our problems for a little while, making us focus our attention on something else, thus giving our minds a much needed break. It is also a great way to counter what happens in the body when we are stressed. Remember that stress causes the body to make hormones. These hormones prepare the body to deal with stress. Exercise helps clear them from our system.

"I think everyone has their own ways of dealing with stress," says Caitlin, age 14. "You're the only one who can help yourself with the stress. I don't think there's anyone like teachers or parents who can make stress easier, it's something we have to learn about and find what works for us."[2]

Running is one type of aerobic exercise. Other examples include kickboxing, swimming, jumping rope, and cycling.

Dealing With Stress

Regular exercise creates a strong body—inside and out. Stress involves the muscles, heart, lungs, and circulation. Exercise improves all of these. It also lowers cholesterol and boosts the immune system. So it counters the effects of the stress response. "During exercise the body releases endorphins, which act as natural anti-depressants and make you feel good," says Dr. Trevor Powell.[3]

Aerobic exercise, or any activity that boosts the heart rate, helps to get rid of adrenaline, noradrenaline, and corticoids made by the adrenal glands. According to Kenneth H. Cooper, M.D., "Our bodies have been designed to eliminate them through active physical channels." He explains, "Aerobic exercise is our most potent modern-day antidote to these destructive accumulations of stress."[4] Getting some exercise into your day doesn't have to be a hassle. Go out for a run or a bike ride. Get a jump rope. Do a few laps in the community pool.

Good Nutrition

Stress slows down digestion. This is one reason the mouth becomes dry. Rather than using energy to digest lunch, the body sends energy to the muscles. Even mild stress will cause the stomach to work more slowly. Instead of eating three large meals, nutritionists suggest eating several smaller meals. Eat healthy snacks between meals. Avoid fatty foods. They are hard to digest even when we are not stressed. Some people get indigestion or heartburn when foods are spicy. During times of stress, avoid these types of food.[5]

Life is busy. Stress adds to this load. Most teens say they feel overwhelmed a lot. Too much to do and not enough time to get it done means eating on the run. We eat whatever is around. We grab sugary snacks, potato chips, and candy bars. We swing by the drive-thru for burgers and fries, or we order pizza for delivery. These foods are all low in nutrition but high in fat, salt, and sugar.

A strong body needs good food to stay healthy. When the body is fit and healthy it can better cope with stress. Diet plays an important role in dealing with stress. A poor diet does not provide the body with enough new energy. A poor diet also depletes energy reserves. After the body burns up all the glucose released during the stress response, it looks for more energy. The choices include stored fat and muscle protein. If it does not get energy from food, it turns first to the muscles. It is faster and easier for the body to break down protein in the muscles than to convert it from fat.[6]

This increases demands on the muscles. The body will feel more stressed because it does not have the strength it needs to cope. Eating protein and complex carbohydrates will provide the energy the body needs. This will keep the body from turning to muscle protein to get energy. Foods such as lean meat, chicken or turkey, fish, low-fat dairy, and beans give the body extra energy. Fruit, pasta, rice, bread, popcorn, and potatoes add complex carbohydrates for quick energy.

This quick energy is better than eating a candy bar. High-sugar foods provide a quick burst of energy that drops quickly. But the body breaks down complex carbohydrates slowly.

Dealing With Stress

It turns them into glucose, which fuels the body. The supply is steady as these foods are slowly converted to maintain the energy level.

"As a result of a complex of physical reactions, the body does not absorb ingested nutrients well when it is under stress," explains Phyllis A. Balch.[7] Stress drains vitamins A, B, and C. The kidneys also make and expel extra calcium, zinc, and magnesium. Plenty of foods will help the body replace these vitamins and minerals.

Oranges and citrus fruits, bell peppers, baked potatoes, yellow fruits and vegetables, and leafy greens are high in vitamins A and C. Whole grains, nuts, and beans supply vitamin B. Calcium is obtained by eating dairy foods and canned sardines with bones, oranges, tofu, and dark green vegetables. Shellfish, liver, wheat germ, sesame seeds, and pumpkin seeds replace lost zinc. Nuts, beans, apricots, artichokes, and soybeans provide magnesium.

Nutritionists and doctors also suggest drinking water; fruit juices; and red, green, or herbal teas when we are stressed. Limit the amount of coffee, black tea, and cola you drink. All of these beverages contain caffeine, which stimulates the adrenal glands. If you are already stressed, this can add to the stress hormones the adrenal glands are supplying to your body. Too much caffeine may cause stomachaches, headaches, a racing

Stress robs your body of the nutrients it needs to run efficiently. Eating healthy foods, such as fresh fruit, will replenish the lost vitamins and minerals and give you the energy to tackle your problems.

or irregular heartbeat, nervousness, poor mental control, insomnia, and panic attacks.

Sugar and salt are also "mood foods." These may make us feel good, but they are not good for us. Too much salt boosts blood pressure. Our blood pressure automatically rises when we are stressed. Adding salty foods can lead to high blood pressure, heart disease, or stroke. Sugar provides short-term energy. Too much sugar when we are stressed can overload the adrenal glands, sapping our strength. In the end, you may have mood swings, have trouble concentrating, and feel cranky and irritable. This is what most people know as a "sugar crash." In addition, indulging in sweet treats too frequently can cause weight gain and tooth decay, which in turn, stresses us out even more.

Instead of heading to "mood foods," try to identify which foods provide you with a comfortable feeling. Comfort foods trigger memories of times when we felt happy, safe, and cared for. We each have different foods that remind us of comfort, such as chicken soup when we had a bad cold, homemade vegetable soup on a cold winter day, grilled cheese sandwiches after playing outside all morning, or steaming oatmeal with cinnamon and raisins on a cool fall morning. Eating them during times of stress may help us feel that same comfort. Though they do not make stress go away, they are a healthy alternative to eating on the go. The "feel good" effect helps improve our attitude while feeding the body.[8]

Nutrition and exercise are only the beginning in taking good care of yourself. Several tools offer an advantage in dealing with stress. Together they keep you healthy—in body and mind.

Rest and Relaxation

The most helpful thing fourteen-year-old Caitlin has found in dealing with stress is "to get a lot of rest and to take things one step at a time."[9]

Sleep is very important. The stress response makes cortisol in the body. "Ordinarily, cortisol is broken down during sleep," says Balch.[10] It is replenished every morning. Ongoing stress does not allow this to happen. The body will reserve it instead. This is why rest and relaxation are important.

Relaxation offsets stress. Just as the body has a stress response, it has a relaxation response to counteract it. It is the opposite of "fight or flight." Blood pressure lowers. The heart rate slows to normal. Tight muscles relax. It is supposed to happen naturally when danger passes. But when we are constantly stressed, it does not always happen. When in distress, you can help bring about the relaxation response.

Simple stretches may be enough. Stretching helps to ease tight muscles. This tells the body that stress has ended. Dr. Kenneth H. Cooper suggests a simple muscle-relaxing exercise. Focus on your toes and feet. "As you focus, practice tightening the muscles throughout your feet and then relaxing them. When the tension has left your feet, move to the muscles in your lower legs, and repeat the exercise."[11] He suggests continuing this process. Your stress will be lower by the time you reach your face.

If you do not have the space to stretch out your body, you can target neck and shoulders. While sitting in a chair, raise your arms above your head. Link your fingers, palms up. Press up as high as you can. Hold for ten seconds. Release. Repeat two or three times. Relax and shake out your arms.

Shoulder shrugs also relieve tension. Raise and then lower your shoulders several times. Now, circle them forward five times. Now, circle them backward five times. Relax. Next, move your head gently from side to side. Now move it forward (chin toward chest) and back (look at the ceiling). Gently rotate your head in circles, first to the left, then to the right.

Dealing With Stress

Breathing exercises also help relieve stress. During times of stress, breathing is short and rapid. People with ongoing stress tend to breath from their chest. The shoulders rise slightly. The belly does not move in and out. Deeper breaths push the belly out. Taking deep breaths helps turn off the stress reaction. The blood receives more oxygen. The body expels carbon dioxide.

Notice how you breathe. Place the palm of one hand on your stomach. Place the other on your chest. Take several deep breaths. Which hand moves more? If the hand on your stomach moves more, you are taking full, deep breaths. If this hand hardly moves, try to breathe from the belly instead.

Simply stretching your arms up above your head while sitting down can help your muscles relax.

Inhale and allow your stomach to extend as the lower lungs fill with air. Count in for three seconds. Count out for three seconds. A few repetitions will help ease tension and loosen you up.

Meditation combines breathing and relaxation. There are different types of meditation. People often think of meditation as boring and requiring a long time to master. You might imagine people sitting in robes for hours repeating a single word. But if you have ever stared into the sky, at the ocean, or into a campfire and "zoned out," you have felt what meditation is all about. Anyone can meditate in any place they feel at peace and at any time they feel like doing it.

Our minds are filled with thoughts and the busyness of daily life. Meditation helps us focus on only one thought. It helps tune out all the other noises and find peace in our mind. It mimics the deep relaxation we might feel just as we fall asleep. But we do not sleep.

The simplest method for meditation is to concentrate on your breathing. Sit in a comfortable position on the floor. Or lie back with your knees bent slightly. Exhale deeply. Inhale deeply. Now allow yourself to breath normally. Notice your breath coming into and leaving your body. As you exhale, notice your breath leaving your lungs. Imagine your breath floating above your body down to your toes. Inhale, and notice the breath fill your lungs. As you breathe in and out, focus on your breath. When thoughts interrupt, allow them to simply float away. Return to focusing on your breathing.[12]

Dealing With Stress

Pamper Yourself

Kelsey had a very difficult first year in high school. She felt very stressed when she came home every day. Evenings were worse as she tried to get homework done. To help deal with this stress, she took breaks from her homework. "I would lie outside on the swing bench and read if the weather was still nice. Then I would go in and start again. If that didn't work, I'd take a bubble bath with some sweet-smelling soaps and shampoos."[13]

Meditating isn't as complicated as it seems. Just going to a local park and breathing in the fresh air can help you clear your head and feel a sense of calm.

Allowing time for yourself is important. When Kelsey sat on the porch, she gave her mind a break. This changed her attitude and mood. She still had a lot of homework to do, but she felt ready to tackle the problem again.

As a way to deal with stress, we can do small things to help improve our moods. Kelsey mentioned sweet-smelling soaps. The scent probably made her feel happy or calm. Perhaps it triggered a good memory. Selecting a favorite perfume or scented oil may also bring comfort.

Healing through the sense of smell is called aromatherapy. The sense of smell is the strongest of our five senses. Unlike the scents in candles, shampoos, and soaps, aromatherapy uses essential oils. These are the essence of plants and flowers. You can buy them at health-food or body-care stores. These oils can be placed in bathwater, rubbed on the skin, or placed over small burners that diffuse the scent into the air.

Different scents are said to have different effects on the body. Some energize while others calm. For example, jasmine, cedarwood, and neroli oils are calming. Sandalwood eases tension and anxiety. Lavender helps treat sleep problems, depression, and high blood pressure. Chamomile is used for stress and sleep difficulties.[14]

The sense of hearing can also help us ease stress. Loud noises and too much audio input

Dealing With Stress

Tips From Teens

When a group of Collier County (Florida) teens were asked what they do to handle their stress, they provided the following list.[15]

- prioritize by making a list of things to do
- exercise, stretch, run, skate, take a walk around the block
- reconnect with the outdoors, spend a day in the sun
- get as much rest as possible
- talk to a parent or close friend
- work on a hobby
- read
- listen to music
- sit in a quiet place
- watch funny shows on TV or tell jokes
- relax

can add to our stress. Turn off the television and turn on the radio or music. Dr. Cooper points to research on using music to relieve anxiety. The studies were done with patients preparing for surgery. "Those who filled their minds with music had significantly less stress and anxiety than did those who weren't exposed to the music."[16]

When Kelsey, fifteen, feels stressed, she plays her cello or listens to music. She also writes in a journal. Between losing friends and having more difficult work, "My first year in high school was the most stressful year of my life," she said. "So I started a journal. It really helped me to write down everything I was feeling, because I can't open up to people easily. I still do it to this day, even if there's nothing to write about. It keeps me in touch with myself."[17]

Sara, nineteen, agrees that getting in touch with yourself is important in maintaining your sanity. "Take some time to yourself away from the influence of others and answer your own questions about why you are feeling the way you feel. Figure out what works best for you as far as dealing with it because no mind is the same. Just do it in a healthy manner."[18]

Essential oils and bath salts are used in aromatherapy.

Laughing and crying can both relieve tension. Crying is a natural release to the build-up of emotion and tension, which is why children cry easily. During the transition from childhood to adolescence, crying is seen as "babyish" behavior, so teens believe they must "hold in" that emotion. Allowing yourself to cry every now and then is a good way to release tension, but keep in mind that excessive crying is also a symptom of stress. Both laughing and crying balance the effects of the fight-or-flight response. However, laughter is better for you. It soothes the nervous system and boosts circulation. It triggers endorphins, the body's natural pain-killers. They also improve mood. Dr. Cooper states: "Humor can act as a distraction or substitute for worry."[19] More than that, joking and laughing with friends can change a bad mood. We feel better when we think positive thoughts.

Talking about problems and having someone to listen also makes us feel better. Some teens have difficulty talking about what stresses them. They may feel that others will view them as silly or weak. "I keep it to myself," says Jessica, fifteen.[20] "I feel like [adults] would judge me if told them." Kelsey, also fifteen, agrees about the difficulty of talking out problems. "My entire life I had kept my emotions bottled up. I learned later it was so much easier just to talk about them in the first place. I still never feel great about opening up to people (it's just something I've always had trouble doing). But once I do, I feel so much better."[21]

Time Management

Keeping yourself organized is also an important tool. When we are stressed, time often feels out of our control. Many teens say they feel overwhelmed or have too much to get done. Time is a resource for dealing with stress. But it will only add to our stress unless we manage it well.

Time management is really about balancing what you want to do with what you have to do. Begin by honestly looking at what must get done in a specific time period. Make a list of the chores, homework, or things you have to do. List when they must be finished. Break down each item into smaller steps. Looking at these steps, decide how to order the list. This is called prioritizing.

"If I have a huge test the next day, I will do 95 percent of my other homework instead of 100 percent," says fifteen-year-old Megan.[22] She then feels she can use some of that time for other tasks.

Suppose you have book a report due at the end of the month but also have a science project due at the end of the week. Prioritize by due date, and you will focus on the science project. You will then have to read the entire book in only a few weeks, then write the report. But if you break these tasks into steps, it will be easier. You might read a few chapters each week, make notes on points to include in the book report, then write it. Each day do a little work on the science project and also read a few chapters of the book. You will not feel a time crunch to get each assignment finished. You will also have time to do some things you enjoy. This helps the mind and body recharge.

When we take too much time to recharge, however, it becomes procrastination. Dr. Trevor Powell defines

Advice for Dealing With Stress

The American Academy of Child & Adolescent Psychiatry offers suggestions to help teens cope with stress.[23]

- Eat and exercise regularly.
- Limit caffeine. Too much can increase restlessness and anxiety.
- Don't use tobacco, alcohol, or illegal drugs.
- Use relaxation exercises, including deep-breathing techniques.
- Learn to stand up for yourself. Practice firm, polite requests ("I feel angry when you speak so critically" or "Please stop shouting at me"). Avoid being either pushy or timid.
- Practice situations that can cause stress. Take a public-speaking class if talking in front of groups causes you stress.
- Learn coping skills, such as breaking large tasks into smaller steps.
- Decrease negative self-talk. Spin negative thoughts into neutral or positive statements. For example, "I'll never pass this class; I'm hopeless at math" becomes "This is difficult, but I can get better at it if I work hard and get some help."
- Learn to feel good about trying your best. Do not expect everything to be perfect.
- Take a break. Do something you enjoy to reduce stress. Swim, bike, or dance. Listen to music or talk to a friend. Draw, write, or sing. Play with a pet.
- Find a group of friends who help you cope with stress.

procrastination as "putting something off that you know you need to do."[24] When we purposely avoid getting started because we cannot face our fears, it becomes a problem. Powell explains that people procrastinate when they worry about failing or someone not approving of the result. They also procrastinate because they worry about succeeding. If they do well, people will expect them to do as well next time. Not liking the task or seeing it as unimportant can also cause people to procrastinate.[25]

The flip side of procrastination is perfectionism. Like procrastination, it keeps us from getting things done. We do not feel it is good enough yet, so we continue working on it. But this extra time and effort may not provide the expected gain. And other things on the list still wait, which adds to the pressure. Perfectionists have not learned to vary their standards based on time available, effort needed, and consequences.[26] Like learning to prioritize, we need to understand which projects can be good enough, good, better, and best.

Your time is managed well when you do both what you must do and also what you want to do. Balancing between fun and work helps ease the stress load. Some of the effects of stress on the body are relieved.[27]

We will always have stress to deal with. It is part of life. But with a strong body and these tools stress can be managed. It does not have to damage the body or cause illness.

When Stress Harms

Our bodies are not designed for ongoing stress. The stress response is supposed to be temporary. The body reacts to a stressor to give us the energy to take action. It is meant to get us through the danger or help us deal with change. Mild or low-grade stress over long periods can wear out the body.

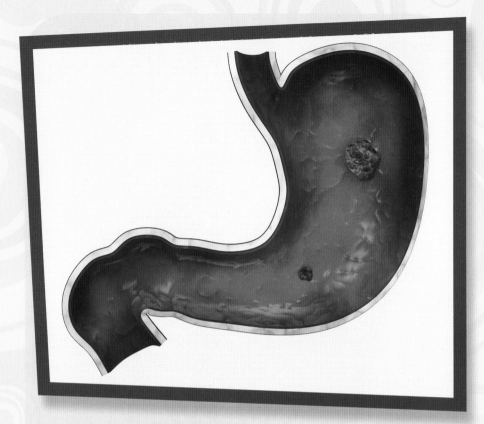

Chronic stress increases your risk of developing stomach ulcers, which are holes in the lining of the stomach. Symptoms include abdominal pain, bloating, vomiting, and loss of appetite.

Even though the body is not on high alert, stress hormones are released, and the body responds to provide extra energy. Our bodies never have a chance to recover. Without relaxation, the body slowly weakens. This continuous state of stress allows illness or disease to take hold. "Researchers estimate that stress contributes to as many as 80 percent of all major illnesses," states nutritionist Phyllis A. Balch.[1] The places where we harbor stress may become a target for illness or disease.

Long-term stress can affect any organ involved in the stress response. Weakened lungs lead to respiratory problems, including bronchitis and asthma. Low or high blood sugar results when the liver is the target. Overworked adrenal glands can lead to diabetes. Heart disease, high blood pressure, and stomach problems such as ulcers can also result from long-term stress. Changes in vision and skin disorders such as acne and dermatitis also result from too much stress.

Stress Load

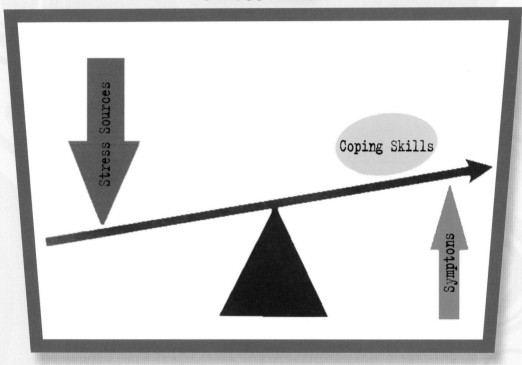

When the demands of life begin to outweigh our ability to cope, we begin to show physical symptoms of stress. The more intense the stress, the more serious the symptoms become.

Checks and Balances

The hypothalamus and amygdala begin the stress response by sending messages to the pituitary gland and the adrenal glands. They also work to regulate the stress response. As cortisol enters the bloodstream, it checks the immune system. When the level of activity in the immune system is good, cortisol sends messages to the brain. The hypothalamus and pituitary gland make adjustments based on those signals. If a boost is needed, more hormones are made. If the body has enough stress hormones, a signal is sent. Fewer hormones are made and sent into the bloodstream.

Cortisol acts like a thermostat. When stress hormones drop, more cortisol is made, just as a thermostat makes the furnace send more heat when the temperature in a house drops. When the level of stress hormones flowing through the blood is too high, less cortisol is made. Cortisol will also send messages when its own levels get too high. It will slow production of hormones from both the hypothalamus and pituitary gland that tell the body to make more cortisol. It also monitors the immune system to prevent inflammation.

"Cortisol's checks-and-balances effect is what makes it such a successful treatment for . . . rashes or allergies," ailments in which the body attacks healthy tissue, says brain researcher and professor Bruce McEwen. "When we put cortisone cream on a rash or take steroids orally to fight inflammation, we are only supplementing what our own cortisol normally does."[2]

When one of the parties in this system of checks and balances is not doing its job, the others may go overboard in doing theirs. For example, if the adrenal glands slow down and there is not enough

cortisol to keep things balanced, the immune system goes wild. Without cortisol acting as a thermostat, the immune system overreacts. It thinks something that is not really a threat may harm the body. This overreaction ends up causing swelling, rashes, and other ailments.

Too much or too little cortisol—or any of the stress hormones—tips the body out of balance. This is when health problems are caused by the stress response. We risk imbalance if stress is ongoing. The same happens when we are bombarded by stressors.

Immune Imbalances

Too little cortisol makes the immune system overreact and attack healthy tissue. This results in inflammation, allergies, and autoimmune disorders.[4] Chronic stress can wear out the thermostat. Even after the emergency is over, cortisol keeps working. Too much cortisol causes the immune system to shut down. Some people under chronic stress always seem to get a lot of colds. It is not their imagination, according to Bruce McEwen.[5] Other types of infection are also possible.

Stress weakens the immune system, making you more susceptible to colds and other infections.

Diabetes

Extreme stress plays a role in diabetes. People who are unable to cope or are bombarded with stressors report feelings of fatigue, lack of energy, irritability, demoralization, and hostility. The body creates excessive cortisol, which dulls the effects of insulin. The body can also become resistant to insulin. Insulin transports glucose into cells, where it is stored. When stress interferes with how insulin functions, glucose builds up in the blood instead of the cells, putting the body at risk for type II or non-insulin-dependent diabetes.[6]

Bones

Cortisol also alters bone mineral density. Making new bone is put on hold, just as digestion slows as part of the fight-or-flight response. Teens involved in sports are at higher risk. Though exercise is encouraged to counter stress, athletes train hard. The extra exercise may not seem stressful, but the body thinks it is under excessive stress. This is especially dangerous for girls. "Results can include weight loss, lack of menstruation, and anorexia, a condition often related to exercise extremism," according to McEwen.[7]

Circulation Problems

Both adrenaline and cortisol play a part in problems with the heart and blood. Too much adrenaline makes blood pressure go up. The heart pumps harder and faster. Eventually, ongoing stress damages the blood vessels in the heart and brain. This damage makes rough spots in the blood vessels. Sticky white blood cells are sent to the rough spot to protect it. Instead, scars build up. These scars are called "lesions." They make the blood vessel narrow so less blood can flow through. This is known as hardening of the arteries. The body is at risk for heart attack or stroke.[8]

Symptoms of Prolonged Stress

When prolonged stress causes the following symptoms, take action to relieve the stress. The warning signs listed on the left can lead to the diseases and conditions on the right.

Symptoms	Diseases/Conditions
anxiety	high blood pressure
restlessness	heart disease
trouble sleeping	asthma
eating disorders	psoriasis
melancholy	eczema
diminished self-esteem	diabetes
	obesity
	depression

The Brain

Cortisol also affects the brain. It can cause problems when the body has too much cortisol. But the brain can also be impaired when the body clock is off. Cortisol works with the body's inner clock, or circadian rhythms. This is related to the way the body responds to light and dark, morning and night. Most of us sleep during the night and rise in the morning. The body requires extra energy to get out of bed and prepare for the day. A boost from the stress hormones helps us shed sleepiness and become alert.

Cortisol and adrenaline both help us wake up. Cortisol works in the brain. Adrenaline works in the body. Throughout the day, these hormones make chemical links with brain cells. This helps us fix important things in our memory.[9] When either hormone is out of balance, we have trouble remembering things. When our circadian rhythm is out of balance, these hormones have to work harder to aid memory and body function.

Excessive stress can cause parts of the body to wear out. One vulnerable part of the brain, the hippocampus, plays two roles in stress. First, it links memory and knowledge. Second, it helps turn off the stress response after danger has passed.[10] The hippocampus is involved in remembering daily events and information, such as shopping lists and names of people, places, and things. It also makes sense out of information such as the time and place of events and the emotions behind them. High levels of stress hormones block the formation and recall of these memories, so that information needed to make a decision or define a problem is not available. When the hippocampus gets worn out from constant stress or damaged due to a head injury, we cannot get accurate information about a stressor, and we cannot properly shut off the stress response. So stress levels rise, which further taxes the body.

Cortisol also works on another part of the brain. The amygdala is important in forming long-term memories that are connected with fearful or traumatic events. This is an area of the brain "scanned" during the body's high alert. Have I ever been in this situation before? How did I feel? What did I do? Can I cope now?

Depression is one mental illness that can result from experiencing too much stress over a long period of time.

"The amygdala is also involved in what we might call anticipatory angst," explains McEwen.[11] This is the anxiety we feel even if there is no real reason to worry. Boosting the stress hormones in this part of the brain makes us even more anxious. And this anxiety causes us to become more stressed.

Sometimes the body does not hear the "all clear." Even after a stressful situation has passed, the body keeps the stress response going. This means the mind can also stay on "high alert," filled with worry and anxiety. Like the body, the

Dealing With Stress

mind does not respond to the all clear. "Most of us can probably remember repeatedly rehashing an argument or other stressful scene, getting worked up all over again until our friends grew tired of hearing about it," states McEwen.[12] He explains that in some people, this is a chronic condition and genes may be involved. Others may need to learn about managing emotions and practicing relaxation to keep the body alert to stress response signals.

Too much cortisol in the body is also a factor in depression. According to McEwen, "People who have had excessive stress in their lives, as measured by multiple episodes of living at the poverty level, show earlier aging, more depression, and an earlier decline of both physical and mental functioning." Excessive stress and abuse in childhood are linked to "an increased risk of depression, suicide, substance abuse, and earlier illness and death from a wide range of diseases."[13]

Long-term overexposure to adrenaline and cortisol causes damage to the body. Sometimes it is due to stress going on too long. Other times the body is wearing out from ongoing stress. It can no longer tell when stress has passed. And sometimes it is because the shutoff process is not working.

How our body responds to stress and whether stress will cause damage depends on our lifestyle. How well do we cope with daily stress. What do we eat? Do we smoke? How well do we sleep? How often do we exercise? The answers to these questions "all feed into the final common path that is the production of cortisol, adrenaline, and other cast members in the allostatic scenario," says McEwen.[14]

A good attitude and using tools for managing stress can keep it from becoming harmful. "I've learned that it will all be okay in the end whether you like it or not," says fourteen-year-old Jessica about outcomes of stressful situations. "I would say that you should think before you act. If you take your time, things will fall into place." She says, "I know a girl who handles [stress] well. Her name is Bailey and she handles her stress by not worrying about it. 'Hakuna Matata,' she says."[15]

Seeking Help

Coping skills will help you learn to deal with stress. But what if they do not seem to work? Sometimes stress can seem to boil over. We feel out of control. Sometimes we watch adults close to us struggle with stress. This can be unsettling. How are teens supposed to be in control when even adults cannot deal with stress? During these times, we need to ask for help. We cannot always deal with our problems alone.

Too much stress can cause overload. If this goes on for too long, it can cause long-term problems. Asthma and diabetes are only two examples. Depression and anxiety disorders can also arise from stress.

Health Risks

When stress goes on too long, our organs and immune system weaken from dealing with it. This is why we catch colds or the flu when we are stressed. If the stress continues, more serious problems develop, such as problems with the heart and blood pressure. Any disease that strikes the skin, liver, lungs, stomach, or intestines can find a foothold in a weakened system.

The mind can also be affected. Some people cannot seem to turn off the worry. They may be overcome by anxiety or depression. Dr. Trevor Powell describes too many demands, too many changes, or loss of any kind as ingredients for depression.[1]

It does not matter how well someone thinks he copes with stress. If stress happens again and again over a long period of time, the whole body suffers.

Family Issues

Some teens feel overwhelmed by stress because of things going on at home. Divorce, a parent looking for work, or an ill relative can add to the regular stress a teen feels. Problems at home are often out of our control. The inability to address a problem can add to the stress load.

> "**It** was very empowering to know that I can choose what is good for me emotionally. Everyone thinks we have to do things as a social obligation, but really, you're the best mediator for yourself and how you are going to feel once in the situation. It's a powerful thing, knowing that you can make your own decisions based on your own feelings, no one else's."
>
> —*Margot, age 17*[2]

"Problems get people down," says Joyce Walker, a 4-H youth development advisor. "We feel tense, fearful, or angry because things are changing—they seem out of control. It's hard to manage."[3] She notes that many teens turn to friends for help when they cannot solve problems themselves. She suggests a five-step plan for helping friends who have turned to them for support, which she calls C-L-U-E-S for short:

- connect
- listen
- understand
- express concern
- seek help

When the problem is big or out of control, Walker says, "Don't agree to be secretive. Enlarge the circle of support."[4] Sometimes the best thing we can do for ourselves or someone we love is to ask for help.

Secondhand Stress

One more type of stress may add to normal stresses teens deal with—secondhand stress. It is triggered by something that happens to someone else. We feel it as if it were happening to us. The symptoms are the same. So is the body's response.

You may experience the stress of friends or family members. You listen to their problems and you try to help. Then you become wrapped up in their stress as well as your own.

There is nothing wrong with trying to help a friend in need, but your friend's problems shouldn't take over your life too.

Dealing With Stress

Danger Signs

Everyone may feel a few of these signs from time to time. But they should not last for long. If they last for longer than a week or two, get help. Also seek help if more than a few are present at once. According to Joyce Walker, a youth development advisor with 4-H, the warning signs include:

- withdrawing from friends, school, and social activities
- obsessing about the problem
- unexpected fits of crying or rage
- insomnia; always feeling drained or in a bad mood
- loss of appetite or vomiting after eating
- always sleeping or daydreaming to forget about the problem
- dramatic change in personality—for example, a usually shy person behaving out of control
- isolation from others
- drug or alcohol abuse

There are four other behaviors that indicate a person is in serious trouble. He could be contemplating suicide if he does the following:

- talks about killing himself
- acts like he is going to die; he might give away things that have meaning to him, prepare a will, or say good-bye to loved ones
- expresses that the future is hopeless and not worth living for
- acts like no one cares about him; he stops caring about himself and others[5]

When you feel like life's problems are consuming you, don't be afraid of turning to your mom or dad for advice. They probably went through the same things when they were teens and learned from those experiences.

Dealing With Stress

"My friends can make bad decisions from time to time," says Kelsey, age fifteen, "and I always feel like it's my responsibility to help them. I'm constantly told that it's not, but I can't help worrying for them."[6]

But secondhand stress can also be triggered by something in the news. It could be an event that hits too close to home, such as a report of a wildfire. It could be something that you can relate to because it is happening to other teens.

Try to notice whether you feel anxious after watching the news on TV or reading the newspaper. Note if you feel more restless or worried after listening to a friend's problems. When dealing with secondhand stress, use the coping skills you've learned for dealing with your own stress.

Teens often do not have control of all the stressors in their lives. Focus on coping with those that are in your control, such as work, school, and friends. Become aware of how you respond to stressors. Learn to see the warning signs of serious stress. And do not be ashamed of asking for help. A friend, a doctor, a trusted teacher or family member, or the school counselor is a great place to start. A doctor may recommend medications to help with anxiety or depression. A doctor or school counselor may refer you for therapy so you will learn how to identify what is causing stress and anxiety. You will feel better if you ask for help because all of these people will listen and can offer ways to help you deal with stress.

Chapter 1. Teens Under Pressure

1. Personal interview with Tyler LeBlance and survey, October 20, 2010.

2. Personal interview with Sara Ardizoni, June 6, 2008.

3. Anita Chandra, DrPH, and Ameena Batada, DrPH, "Exploring Stress and Coping Among Urban African American Adolescents: The Shifting the Lens Study," *Preventing Chronic Disease*, vol. 3, no. 2, April 2006, p. 4.

4. Personal interview with Margot Ehaglund, June 5, 2008.

5. Personal interview with Megan Wheeler, June 6, 2008.

6. U.S. Department of Health and Human Services, *The Surgeon General's Call to Action to Prevent and Reduce Underage Drinking* (Rockville, Md.: Office of the Surgeon General, 2007), p. 16, <http://www.surgeongeneral.gov/topics/underagedrinking/calltoaction.pdf> (April 14, 2011).

7. Personal interview with Hunter Leake III, MD, February 14, 2011.

8. Aaron T. Ebata, PhD, "Helping Young Adolescents Cope With Stress," *National Network for Child Care*, March 1996, <http://www.nncc.org/SACC/sac42_adolesc.stress.html> (May 30, 2008).

9. Candace Brown, survey/questionnaire, June 7, 2008.

10. Survey and interviews, Naples, Florida, June 4-6, 2008, and October 16-20, 2010.

11. Chandra and Batada, p. 4.

12. Ibid., p. 5.

13. Jennifer Dyl, PhD, "Helping Young Adolescents Cope With Stress," *Lifespan*, n.d., <http://www.lifespan.org/services/childhealth/parenting/teen-stress.htm> (May 9, 2008).

Chapter 2. The Body on High Alert

1. Survey and interviews, Naples, Florida, June 4-6, 2008, and October 16-20, 2010.

2. Bruce S. McEwen and Elizabeth Norton Lasley, *The End of Stress as We Know It* (Washington, D.C.: Joseph Henry Press, 2002), pp. 22–23.

3. Personal interview with Samantha Bodnar, October 19, 2010.

4. Personal interview with Hunter Leake III, MD, February 14, 2011.

5. McEwen and Lasley, p. 24.

6. Phyllis A. Balch, CNC, *Prescription for Herbal Healing* (New York: Penguin Group, 2002), p. 404.

7. McEwen and Lasley, pp. 21–24.

8. Phyllis A. Balch, CNC, *Prescription for Natural Healing,* 4th ed. (New York: Penguin Group, 2006), p. 721.

Chapter 3. Who Needs Stress?

1. Aaron T. Ebata, PhD, "Helping Your Adolescents Cope With Stress," *National Network for Child Care,* March 1996, <http://www.nncc.org/SACC/sac42_adolesc.stress.html> (May 30, 2008).

2. Frederic Friedman, "Questions About Stress," *Lifespan*, n.d., <http://www.lifespan.org/services/mentalhealth/articles/stress/stress_questions.htm> (May 9, 2008).

3. Personal interview with Colvin Warburton, October 16, 2010.

4. Electronic interview with Margot Ehaglund, June 5, 2008.

Chapter 4. What Stresses You Out?

1. Personal interview with Sara Ardizoni, June 6, 2008.

2. Electronic interview with Kelsey Finn, June 7, 2008.

3. Electronic interview with Caitlin Calhoun, June 4, 2008.

4. Anita Chandra, DrPH, and Ameena Batada, DrPH, "Exploring Stress and Coping Among Urban African American Adolescents: The Shifting the Lens Study," *Preventing Chronic Disease*, vol. 3, no. 2, April 2006, p. 4.

5. Personal interview with Colvin Warburton, October 16, 2010.

6. Megan S., survey, June 7, 2008.

7. Caroline, survey, June 7, 2008.

8. U.S. Department of Health and Human Services, *The Surgeon General's Call to Action to Prevent and Reduce Underage Drinking* (Rockville, Md.: Office of the Surgeon General, 2007), p. 20, <http://www.surgeongeneral.gov/topics/underagedrinking/calltoaction.pdf> (April 14, 2011).

9. Survey and interviews, Naples, Florida, June 4-6, 2008 and Brent W., October 17, 2010.

10. Phyllis A. Balch, CNC, *Prescription for Natural Healing*, 4th ed. (New York: Penguin Group, 2006), p. 722.

11. Chandra and Batada, p. 1.

12. Bruce S. McEwen and Elizabeth Norton Lasley, *The End of Stress as We Know It* (Washington, D.C.: Joseph Henry Press, 2002), p. 23.

13. Reader's Digest editors, *The Stress Factor* (Pleasantville, N.Y.: The Reader's Digest Association, 1995), p. 11.

14. Ibid.

15. Aaron T. Ebata, PhD, "Helping Your Adolescents Cope With Stress," *National Network for Child Care,* March 1996, <http://www.nncc.org/SACC/sac42_adolesc.stress.html> (May 30, 2008).

16. Ibid.

17. Personal interview with Sara Ardizoni, June 6, 2008.

18. Ebata.

19. *The Stress Factor,* p. 72.

20. Ibid., p. 75.

21. Ebata.

22. Survey and interviews, Naples, Florida, October 16-20, 2010.

23. Ebata.

Chapter 5. The Problem With Not Coping

1. Anita Chandra, DrPH, and Ameena Batada, DrPH, "Exploring Stress and Coping Among Urban African American Adolescents: The Shifting the Lens Study," *Preventing Chronic Disease,* vol. 3, no. 2, April 2006, p. 7.

2. Electronic interview with Kelsey Finn, June 7, 2008.

3. Survey and interviews, Naples, Florida, October 16-20, 2010.

4 Jessica S., survey, June 6, 2008.

5. Personal interview with Sara Ardizoni, June 6, 2008.

6. U.S. Department of Health and Human Services, *The Surgeon General's Call to Action to Prevent and Reduce Underage Drinking* (Rockville, Md.: Office of the Surgeon General, 2007), p. 21, <http://www.surgeongeneral.gov/topics/underagedrinking/calltoaction.pdf> (April 14, 2011).

7. Personal communication with Dr. Debi Yohn, July 27, 2008.

8. Trevor J. Powell, *Stress Free Living* (London: Dorling Kindersley Limited, 2000), p. 32.

9. Cara DiMarco, PhD, *Moving Through Life Transitions With Power and Purpose,* 2nd ed. (Upper Saddle River, N.J.: Prentice Hall, 2000), p. 50.

10. Ibid., p. 67.

11. Ibid., p. 74.

12. Powell, p. 104.

13. Personal interview with Sara Ardizoni, June 6, 2008.

14. "What Is Stress?" *Child and Youth Health,* n.d., <http://www.cyh.com/HealthTopics/HealthTopicsDetails.aspx?p=240&np=298&id=2082> (May 9, 2008).

15. Personal interview with Sara Ardizoni, June 6, 2008.

16. "What Is Stress?"

17. Chandra and Batada, p. 7.

18. Ibid.

Dealing With Stress

Chapter 6. How to Manage Your Stress

1. Survey and interviews, Naples, Florida, June 6-8, 2008, and October 16-20, 2010.

2. Personal interview with Caitlin Calhoun, June 4, 2008.

3. Trevor J. Powell, *Stress Free Living* (London: Dorling Kindersley Limited, 2000), p. 132.

4. Kenneth H. Cooper, *Can Stress Heal?* (Nashville, Tenn.: T. Nelson Publishers, 1997), p. 82.

5. Reader's Digest editors, *The Stress Factor* (Pleasantville, N.Y.: The Reader's Digest Association, 1995), p. 27.

6. Ibid., p. 26.

7. Phyllis A. Balch, CNC, *Prescription for Natural Healing,* 4th ed. (New York: Penguin Group, 2006), pp. 721–722.

8. *The Stress Factor,* p. 27.

9. Personal interview with Caitlin Calhoun, June 4, 2008.

10. Phyllis A. Balch, CNC, *Prescription for Herbal Healing* (New York: Penguin Group, 2002), p. 404.

11. Cooper, p. 137.

12. Martha Davis, PhD, Elizabeth Robbins Eshelman, MSW, and Matthew McKay, PhD, *The Relaxation and Stress Reduction Workbook,* 5th ed. (Oakland, Calif.: New Harbinger Publications, 2000), pp. 35–41.

13. Electronic interview with Kelsey Finn, June 7, 2008.

14. *The Stress Factor,* p. 68.

15. Survey and interviews, Naples, Florida, June 6-8, 2008, and October 16-20, 2010.

16. Cooper, p. 145.

17. Electronic interview with Kelsey Finn, June 7, 2008.

18. Personal interview with Sara Ardizoni, June 6, 2008.

19. Cooper, p. 149.

20. Personal interview with Jessica Steuber, June 6, 2008.

21. Electronic interview with Kelsey Finn, June 7, 2008.

22. Personal interview with Megan Schultz, June 6, 2008.

23. American Academy of Child and Adolescent Psychiatry, "Helping Teenagers With Stress," *Facts for Families,* no. 66, May 2005, <http://www.aacap.org/page.ww?section=Facts%20for%20Families&name=Helping%20Teenagers%20With%20Stress> (May 9, 2008).

24. Powell, p. 98.

25. Ibid., p. 98.

26. Ibid., p. 99.

27. Ibid., pp. 94–99.

Chapter 7. When Stress Harms

1. Phyllis A. Balch, CNC, *Prescription for Natural Healing,* 4th ed. (New York: Penguin Group, 2006), p. 721.

2. Bruce S. McEwen and Elizabeth Norton Lasley, *The End of Stress as We Know It* (Washington, D.C.: Joseph Henry Press, 2002, pp. 24–25).

3. Scott, survey and interview, October 17, 2010.

4. McEwen and Lasley, p. 25.

5. Ibid., p. 58.

6. Ibid., p. 62.

7. Ibid., pp. 61–62.

8. Ibid., p. 25.

9. Ibid.

10. Ibid., p. 62.

11. Ibid., p. 63.

12. Ibid., pp. 60–61.

13. Ibid., p. 59.

14. Ibid., p. 65.

15. Personal interview with Jessica Johnson, June 7, 2008.

Chapter 8. Seeking Help

1. Trevor J. Powell, *Stress Free Living* (London: Dorling Kindersley Limited, 2000), pp. 24–25.

2. Personal interview with Margot Ehaglund, June 5, 2008.

3. Joyce Walker, "Teens in Distress: Helping Friends in Trouble: Stress, Depression and Suicide," *University of Minnesota*, 2005, <http://www.extension.umn.edu/distribution/youthdevelopment/DA2787.html> (May 18, 2008).

4. Ibid.

5. Ibid.

6. Electronic interview with Kelsey Finn, June 7, 2008.

Glossary

acute stress—Intense type of stress that takes place immediately but also passes quickly.

adrenaline—First of the major stress hormones made by the adrenal glands. Also called epinephrine.

adrenocorticotropic hormone (ACTH)—A chemical made by the pituitary gland that triggers release of stress hormones in the body.

allostasis—A body's response to stress.

chronic stress—Ongoing stress that wears on the body over a long period of time.

corticotrophin-releasing factor (CRF)—A chemical made by the hypothalamus to alert the pituitary gland of stress.

cortisol—Second of the major stress hormones made by the adrenal glands.

distress—A negative type of stress in which normal routines constantly change, so the body and mind must keep adjusting. The body is emotionally stressed by the changes.

endorphin—A painkilling chemical released by the brain during stress.

epinephrine—A stress hormone made by the adrenal glands. Also known as adrenaline.

eustress—A helpful type of stress that prepares the heart, muscles, and mind for strength needed to take action.

exhaustion—Third stage of allostasis when the body has been under stress so long that it wears out or becomes ill.

fight-or-flight response—First stage of allostasis when the body is on high alert.

hippocampus—Center in the brain that stores memories and learning or knowledge related to those memories.

hormones—Chemicals made in the body to provide signals or messages to the brain or organs.

hypothalamus—A tiny section of the brain that handles many body functions such as temperature, sleep, and appetite.

pituitary gland—An almond-sized gland at the front of the brain that makes hormones.

resistance—Second stage of allostasis when the ongoing stress causes the body to fight against, or resist, the stressor.

stressor—A trigger that causes the stress response.

Hotlines

These national organizations offer help to teens:

National Youth Crisis Hotline

    800-442-4673

National Runaway Switchboard (also called the National Adolescent Suicide Hotline)

    800-786-2929

Further Reading

Hipp, Earl. *Fighting Invisible Tigers: A Stress Management Guide for Teens*. Minneapolis, Minn.: Free Spirit Publishing, 2008.

Hyde, Margaret O., and Elizabeth H. Forsyth. *Stress 101: An Overview for Teens*. Minneapolis, Minn.: Twenty-First Century Books, 2008.

Jones, Jami L. *Bouncing Back: Dealing With the Stuff Life Throws at You*. New York: Franklin Watts, 2007.

Reber, Deborah. *Chill: Stress-reducing Techniques for a More Balanced, Peaceful You*. New York: Simon Pulse, 2008.